Skipper

CRAIG B. BASS

ISBN: 978-1-64314-559-4 (Paperback)
978-1-64314-560-0 (Hardback)
978-1-64314-561-7 (E-book)

AUTHORS PRESS

AuthorsPress
California, USA
www.authorspress.com

Contents

PART 1

PART 2

PART 3

PART 4

PART 5

PART 6

PART 7

Life After Skipper And The Scouts

PART 1

CHAPTER 1

INTRODUCTION

THE PERFECTLY BEAUTIFUL DAY could not possibly have been more deceptive in the mind of the boy. Deceptive because, for the unimaginable changes that would soon be occurring to him and his perfect life; a large, dark tornado on the horizon, skipping rapidly, and inexorably toward him would have been more appropriate.

It was early on a Monday morning. The rising sun was already making it warmer in the car. The man and the boy were the only occupants. They were returning from the central Florida ranch, where they had spent the weekend. They had been driving for the past hour. They were running a few minutes late. The boy had to be in school in another hour. In his mind he was reviewing his routine of preparations for departure to school. As they approached his house, they could see an unknown, strange new car in the driveway. It was parked behind his mother's older model Ford car.

"Do you know whose car that is?" asked the man"

No. It's too early for friends on a school day." said the boy.

A look of apprehension appeared on the man's face.

"This may not be good." he said.

"Why is that Skipper?" asked the boy as he searched the man's face.

"It depends on who that is." the man said.

"Who could it be that it's not good?" asked the boy.

"I don't know. I guess it's just a feeling I have. You will know in a few minutes. You better get going, or you will be late. I'll call you tonight after work and see what you found out." said Skipper.

After the boy closed the door of the car, he leaned in through the window.

"I wish we were back on the boat right now Skipper; heading out to go fishing in the Gulf."

"Me too, Greg. Me too! Come next weekend, that's exactly where we will be, and what we will be doing." said Skipper.

As Greg started backing out of the car window Skipper said,

"Greg, I just want you to know, and to remember always how much I care for you, all the boys really, but especially you."

"I care for you too, Skipper. I'll wait for your call tonight." said Greg, with a warm smile.

Greg watched until Skipper's car disappeared from his sight, and then he went inside.

CHAPTER 2

TWO MEN

When Greg opened the front door and entered the living room, he saw two strange men. They were sitting on the couch talking to his mother and her husband. He walked into the room.

"Hi mom, I know I'm a little late, but I'll definitely get to school on time." Greg said. There was no smile on anyone's face.

"Greg, these gentlemen are here to talk to you."

"What about? They are having a special general assembly this morning. They're supposed to be making an announcement about a change in school policy. I shouldn't miss it." Greg said.

"These men are here to talk to you about Skipper. They think it is important enough for you to miss school." His mother said.

"Then, It must be important." Greg said.

He sat down opposite the two men. Both men were wearing dark suits and ties. The man on Greg's right said,

"Greg, I am Bill Fanshaw, my partner here is Gary Thompson. We work for the United States Government. We do investigative work. We are here talking to you because we're investigating some serious complaints about your scout master Skipper."

Greg suddenly felt a sensation of apprehension.

"What kind of complaints?" he asked, as he remembered what Skipper said a few moments earlier.

"Greg, do you know a boy by the name of Matthew Rogers?" Fanshaw asked.

"Yes." answered Greg. He could feel his apprehension mounting.

"How do you know him?"

"Matt's in my scout troop. He's a buddy, or was a buddy. He spends as much time at the ranch as I do." Greg said.

"How long have you known him?"

"About two and a half years. Since I joined the scout troop." said Greg.

"How much time do you spend at the ranch?" asked Gary Thompson.

"Only on weekends, now that school has started. During summers, more of the time." Greg answered.

"Do other boys stay at the ranch with you?" Fanshaw asked.

"Sure, there's usually four of us during summers." said Greg

"How long have you been going to the ranch?" Fanshaw asked.

"About two years, more or less." said Greg.

"Why don't you tell us more about the ranch. Who goes there, what do you do there, how do you spend your time when you're there?" said Gary Thompson.

"We fish, we camp out, we build things, we work on our merit badges, we explore in the swamps and lakes, help take care of the animals; things like that. Last summer there was Matt, Tommy, Bobby and me. Mrs. Parker and Lindsey live there full time. Skipper is there on most weekends. During the summer, he spent two weeks at the ranch. That was when we first started building the boat." Greg said.

"Who decides which boys stay there?" asked Fanshaw.

"Skipper's our scout master, he owns the ranch. So I guess it's him. He always asks us boys what we think about new boys, so maybe it's really all of us." said Greg. Then he added, "May I please ask what this is all about?"

"Greg, one of the scouts claims Skipper has been molesting you." Fanshaw said.

"Doing what?" asked Greg.

"Touching you on your private parts." his mother said. Looking at him with a worried expression on her face.

Greg felt a sudden shock as the adrenalin surged through him.

"It's not true! Who said that? It's not true!" He exclaimed.

"It's not important now, who said it. What is important is if it ever happened." said Gary Thompson.

"It did not happen! I've never seen anything like that going on. Never!"

Both the men, his mother and his step-father were studying his face.

"You are certain you have never seen Skipper touch you or any other boy on the genitalia?" asked Fanshaw.

"Yes! I'm certain. I spend as much time with the other boys and Skipper, and at the ranch as anybody. I have never seen any thing wrong going on at the ranch." Proclaimed Greg.

"All right Greg, that's all we need to ask you, for now. We may need to talk again, but that does it for now." said Gary Thompson.

After the two men left, his mother said,

"Greg, this is all very disturbing. You can tell me the truth, now that they're gone."

"Mom, you don't have to be disturbed. I'm telling you. Nothing wrong ever happened." said Greg

"O.K., son, that's so good to hear. You can get ready and go on to school now." said his mother.

CHAPTER 3

THE PAST

THE SKIPPER DID NOT call that night, nor the next night, and not the next nights. During those days he waited for Skipper to call, Greg remembered and thought about the times before and after meeting Skipper. This led him to think about the months and years of his life around the time of meeting him.

He was two months into the seventh grade, when he decided to join the boy scouts. The troop he chose was at the Elks Club building. It was one block from his mother's beauty shop. It was an ideal location because he would be close to where she worked. He could meet with her before the troop began the nights activities. Since being back from boarding school, and his summer adventures in Georgia, he was looking for better ways to spend his time. His mother and stepfather both worked long hours, and he was alone after school was out, and early into the evenings. He spent a lot of time at the library, but he was looking for some additional activities to occupy his time and energy. He had no friends yet. He was still new to the neighborhood.

He had spent the sixth grade in the catholic boarding school where he also spent the third and fourth grades. His mother and father had divorced when he was four years old. In the early part of the third grade he sustained a laceration that required stitches. It happened while he was playing after school. He was eight years old when it happened, and as there was no one to look after him when school was over, he had been injured while playing on his own. Because of this, and other reasons, he was sent to the catholic boarding school early in the third grade.

He, in ignorance, had used the condoms he found in her boy friend's glove compartment to make balloons out of at a neighbor hood birthday party. This behavior was reported to his mother. As his mother was involved in a relationship with a new man in her life; it seemed obvious now that having a young boy around, who was often in the way and causing trouble, was not ideal for her new relationship. Her boy friend offered to pay for Greg's expenses at a boarding school.

Starting at eight years old, Greg spent the next two years, away from home, at a catholic boarding school. He spent the third and fourth grades, away from his mother, father, and all family members. He remembered that shortly after he arrived at the boarding school, he spent many hours alone; of being curled up on the floor, behind the study hall piano, suffering from severe abdominal pain.

During the fifth grade he lived with his mother and her new husband. That was a busy and turbulent year for him. Before they moved to California for the first time, he was in two different public schools, and lived in three different apartments. They were one bedroom and one bath apartments, so Greg slept on the living room couch.

He thought of this year fondly. It was so much better than boarding school life. He felt that now, at least he had some freedoms again. He could go to the local playgrounds and watch the games they played there. He was not required to account for every moment of his day. At one time he and another friend planned to build a raft. They wanted to float down the Hillsborough River, and be free like Huckleberry Finn.

When they went to California for the first time they rode a greyhound bus. After they arrived in San Diego, they lived with his mother's sister and her husband. He was a successful butcher. They had a three bed room and two bath house, and Greg enjoyed having his own bedroom for the first time in his life. The privacy that went with it was a new experience for him. He found that he enjoyed being alone, and having his own bed at night. When his aunt and uncle moved to another house, Greg and his mother and her husband moved with them. Because of this move he attended two more different schools. In the last school, he only went to classes in the afternoons. The school had to have two school sessions per day, because of their being too many students.

After a few months, Greg and his mother rode the greyhound bus back to Tampa, Florida. Greg thought there was some problem between his mother and her husband. The problem apparently, was over another woman, and it must have happened after his stepfather moved north to Fresno, California looking for better work.

Once they were back in Tampa, his mother and he lived in a small one bedroom second floor apartment on Central Avenue. The apartment was only a few blocks away from the public school Greg attended for the last part of the fifth grade. His mother got a job in a beauty shop in Sulphur Springs. What Greg remembered and liked most about that period of his life, was swimming in the Sulphur Springs swimming pool.

He also remembered seeing his father more than he had ever seen him before, and he liked that. He was around the apartment much of the time. He was eating and sleeping there. Greg enjoyed the time he got to spend with his father during this period. They all seemed to get along fine, for a while, then he realised that gradually something seemed to be going wrong, and his father did not stay with them any more. He never knew what it was that went wrong.

When the school year was over, Greg and his mother got back on the Greyhound bus for another ten-day trip to California. This time they went straight to Bakersfield, where his stepfather was now living. He had a new job selling used cars.

CHAPTER 4

CALIFORNIA

When they first arrived in Bakersfield they lived in a motel room. It was on the eastern outskirts of the city. They lived there for several weeks. During this time Greg entertained himself most days by drawing cartoon characters he copied from the newspaper. He went swimming some days in the nearby public pool, this was his favorite past time, he loved the water and he loved swimming. On some nights all three of them sat around in the motel room listening to the radio. It was activated by depositing coins in the slots on the radio. On more than one occasion the timer on the pay slot expired just minutes before the program was over, and they never got to hear the end of the story. Depositing another coin, just to hear a few more moments and the ending, was not a financial consideration in those days.

After several weeks they all three moved in to the middle of the city. Their apartment was across the street from a public playground. It was only three blocks from the public library. This was good for Greg, because reading was one of his favorite past times, and there was no swimming pool available. With in a few weeks Greg got a job selling news papers on the main streets of Bakersfield. He developed a routine where he sold his papers in the first half of the day. He made enough money to spend the afternoons in movie theaters; where for nine cents he could sit in air conditioning and watch a double feature. On special days he bought popcorn and a soft drink. It only cost him nine cents for the two movies; so on some days he would watch two different double features.

On certain occasions when he needed another penny or two to pay his way in to the movie houses, he would borrow or more commonly steal them from his mother's penny stash. Stealing in this manner evolved easily for Greg, and soon extended to include more items as he met new friends.

He found that the boys who played sports on the playground across the street from his apartment, were exclusively black. His mother who had been born and raised in Florida, and had spent all of her life there, was extremely prejudiced against Negroes. During all of her life in Florida the Negroes had separate public rest rooms, and their own separate water fountains. They always rode in the back of the bus and the trolley cars. They were considered inferior to whites. She could not accept the fact that in California, there was no segregation, and she had to share facilities and transportation with people she considered inferior to her. She even found it difficult to use a public bathroom if a black woman had used it before her.

She also found it necessary to frequently remind Greg about his playmates across the street,

"It is all right with me if you play with them, over there, but don't ever bring one home." she would say this emphatically, and frequently. It did not make any difference to Greg if they were a different color from himself he soon discovered. They were the only boys he had to play with. Besides that they were much better at all of the sports than he was. They were faster, stronger, swifter, and better coordinated than he was; he felt fortunate they did not discriminate against him. They let him, a white boy, play with them, even though he was not very good at any of the sports, and he was grateful to them for that.

This experience made him realize his mother was completely wrong about people with different skin color being inferior to white skinned people. The coloured boys he met were much superior to himself.

As the summer progressed he eventually met some white boys at the movies on Saturday mornings. They were more nearly his age, but, they played different kinds of games. They soon introduced him to some non sporting activities with which he was unfamiliar. Besides going into the nearby bakery where they pilfered fresh loafs of bread when no one was looking, he also learned from them how much fun it was to throw rocks at the passing trains. The train tracks were only two blocks from his apartment. Some times when the trains were stationary they would try to break into the coaches, and when the trains were not moving, it was much easier to shatter the windows with their rocks.

When these types of activities became old and boring, they moved on to seeing who could steal the most from the department stores without getting caught. They especially liked things like pocket knives, and other small items which they could easily slip into their pockets, and leave the store undetected. These types of smaller merchandise were their primary targets, and afterwards they liked to show off among themselves the items they had stolen.

It wasn't long before the managers of the stores became aware of their losses. They increased their surveillance and hired trained spotters to catch the thieves. Greg was fairly successful until one day the manager of his favorite store for stealing, caught him red handed with a knife in his pocket, and one in his hand. This manager made Greg take him straight home to his mother. The manager told Greg's mother he had been suspicious of Greg for a time, because he was seen in the store frequently and he never bought anything. The manager made it very clear that if Greg was seen in the store again, the police would be called and formal charges would be filed.

The very next day, the police saw him walking by the train tracks, they picked him up and took him in to the police station. His mother and stepfather were required to come in to the police station. Greg had been positively identified by train personnel as one of the gang members who were breaking in to parked trains, and shattering moving train windows with rocks. It was finally agreed by his parents and the police, after sufficiently scaring him with threats of incarceration, that he would be let off this time with a warning. It was also in the agreement, Greg would be placed in strict house confinement for three weeks. In addition, if any further problems were reported, he would go before a judge and be recommended for incarceration in a juvenile detention facility. These events and the discovery of the dwindling penny supply led his mother to also realize that Greg had also been stealing from her all this time.

It happened that his grandmother died with in a week of these last events. It was his father's mother, and until she died, she was the only grandmother he had ever known. His other grandmother died when he was an infant. He had always loved his grandmother very much, because she showed how much she loved spending time with her grandson. Both his mother and father worked most days and nights, so he spent many days and nights with his grandmother, at her large house. He could remember the two of them having to climb under the bed together when the sirens wailed, warning of a possible bomb attack by the Japanese and the Germans. She had also taken care of him many times before he was ever sent off to the boarding school. She rode a large tricycle around her property, and to the grocery store sometimes Greg heard people say she had a type of creeping paralysis. When she died she left a small inheritance to Greg in her will. Upon considerations between his father and his mother, it was determined there was enough money left to Greg by his grand mother, to pay for another year at the catholic boarding school. They agreed that it was important to get Greg out of California, and back into a stricter, controlled environment.

Greg and his mother were aboard a Greyhound bus; heading back to Tampa, before the three weeks of confinement was over. They arrived in Tampa in time for him to be installed into the all too familiar routines of the catholic boarding school, which he had previously learned to dislike and dread so much. His year of freedom was over. It had been a busy and adventurous year. He had travelled to California twice. By riding on a Greyhound bus, he got to see the geography between Florida and California with his own eyes. He was in five different schools during the fifth grade, so he had experienced more in one year than most boys.

He remembered his marathon movie days fondly. He loved having his mind being captured, and taken away to new and strangely different places by the magic of the movies. He had now lost all of that freedom.

CHAPTER 5

DIFFERENT DREAMS

ON THE BUS RIDE back to Florida, and returning to the boarding school, he experienced different kinds of dreams for the first time. At night when every one else was trying to sleep, he entertained himself with fantasies and dreams of a graphically sexual, and sometimes aggressive nature. He could not recall the exact fantasies now, but he knew they had something to do with older women holding him down and doing strange things to him. Sometimes they made him do strange things to himself. Exactly what kinds of things he did not remember, but he did know they were stimulating to him. Each night he became eager for the darkness to come. He hoped all the other bus passengers would go to sleep early, so that he could visit those secret and stimulating places of his imaginations and dreams. He was aware these images could not be shared with others. They did not scare him, he actively sought them so that he could draw them forth, and enjoy the stimulation he felt from them.

He also remembered that it was in the fifth grade, when he lived with his mother in Tampa that he had begun to explore his own body with his fingers; trying to discover how things worked, and how it felt when he used his fingers to explore each orfice of his body. Perhaps that was somehow associated with these dreams, because they also were sticking things in him. It was also at this same time when he and his cousin, who was the same age, experimented with each other. While taking a bath together one night his cousin developed an erection, upon both of them becoming aware of the development, his cousin announced with a big grin, "It got hard."

"His tiny pee-pee did get firm and stick up in the air." Greg remembered.

That night, after they went to bed, the boys experimented with each other. They touched each other. They placed their mouth around the others penis. They discovered quickly it was no fun. They never experimented again.

CHAPTER 6

BOARDING SCHOOL YEAR

WHEN THE SIXTH GRADE classes began at the boarding school that year, Greg found he was the oldest of the boys. He was the only boy in the sixth grade. The boarding school took only first through the sixth grades. It was different this year for Greg, because his classes were in the St Anthony schoolhouse in San Antonio, instead of the lovely tree shaded, beautiful, peaceful building on the shore of Lake Jovita.

In the third and fourth grades, the classrooms he attended were in the building located on the edge of the beautiful lake, two hundred yards from the main campus buildings. There were wooden docks extending out from the shore, over the water. The lake was where the boys swam during scheduled play time. When he was in class those days, he could look out over the lake. It was tranquil and peaceful during classes when no one was misbehaving.

His teachers were Sisters of the Benedictine order, and they managed the boarding schools, the boys and the girls Across the street from the boys dormitory was a boarding school for girls. The girl's school boarded students through the twelfth grade. The boys always ate their meals at a table of six with one of the older girls. The older girls functioned as a behavior monitor, and they were in charge of the portion servings.

The sisters were very strict and tolerated little to no misbehavior, particularly in the classroom.

It only took two examples of their management style and the techniques they used for defiant and rebellious boys, to convince Greg to keep his own misbehavior to a minimum. This was not always easy for an eleven year old boy who had experienced unprecedented freedom only a couple of months before.

The first incidence that impressed Greg so much was near the beginning of the school year. It involved another boy who was one year younger than himself. Greg and the other boy were engaged in shooting spit-balls through a straw. They blew the tightly packed, wet paper spit balls at one another, at some of the other students, and at the ceiling. They were having fun, laughing and giggling at each other; blowing the spit-balls at the ceiling, feeling triumphant when a spit-ball stuck. Every one in the class was keeping score. They did their best not to be observed by the teacher, who was a large stout sister with no sense of humor.

Unfortunately she caught the other boy in the active process of shooting a spit-ball at Greg. Greg always tried to fire off his shots when the sister was not looking. The sister called the other boy up to the front of the room for a verbal reprimand, and the traditional three rulers stacked together punishment. The three rulers were used to smack the open palm of the offenders outreached palm, ten times. Greg watched nervously. He had to under go the painful procedure many times previously. The other boy chose to ignore the sister, and to run around the room, and away from her, taunting her with," nanh, nanh a-na na, you can't catch me."

Greg sat frozen in fear to his seat, as he watched. She was a large, rather chubby, stout person, but she moved much faster than any one expected, and she did corner and catch him more quickly than anyone expected. When she did catch him, she turned him upside down, and grabbed him by the ankles. Greg watched intently, somewhat horrified as she began to swing him around and around her, much as any adult would do when playing with a small child for fun. He counted three times around; then she suddenly let him go. The boy, now suddenly released from the force of the hands restraining him back, flew straight through the air several feet, before gravity overcame his horizontal direction, and the downward arc began. This direction brought him quickly in to contact with the floor. He was still moving rather fast, when he made contact with the floor, Greg watched his body slide smoothly on the polished floor, going head first across the slick surface.

Then, he hit the wall. There was a type of muffled smacking sound when he hit the wall. He came to an abrupt stop. He did not get up. He did not even move. The sister calmly walked over to him, where the wall had abruptly stopped his quick slide. She leaned over him. She felt his neck for something, confirmed to her satisfaction he was still breathing, and left him lying there on the floor where he had come to rest. She slowly stood up to her full and imposing height. She looked confidently around the class room, and asked, loudly,

"Does any body else want to get the same treatment?"

The entire class shook their heads in the negative, but did not look up from their desk. The sister then resumed teaching class. In about fifteen or twenty minutes, Greg guessed, the boy sat up slowly, and looked around the room still somewhat dazed. She instructed him to go back to his seat, which he promptly, but slowly did. He did it without muttering another word, and without looking at the sister.

The other significant incident happened in study hall, just before dinner, one afternoon. Greg was sitting next to Bernaise Folgers. Bernaise was one of his closest friends that year. Bernaise was hiding his face from the sister who sat in the front of the room. His face was hidden behind a sheet of paper he was holding in front of him. He was hiding the fact that he was looking at Greg, making funny faces, and trying to make Greg laugh. He was making a really funny face, trying hard to get Greg to laugh at him. Greg was looking directly at Bernaise, when he saw the ruler cut through the sheet of paper. It immediately emerged as a blur from the paper hiding Bernaise's face. The end of the ruler struck him in the middle of the forehead. The force knocked him out of his seat, on to the floor, and into the aisle, at Greg's feet. Greg immediately looked toward the front of the class room.

The sister was still still standing in the stance from which she had launched the ruler. She now looked in his direction. Greg immediately looked down and resumed his homework. The sister walked calmly down the aisle to where Bernaise lay on the floor, she helped him back in to his seat, examined his forehead which was by now swelling and beginning to form a moderate sized lump. Apparently satisfied, she stood up and announced to the group in general, "There is no tom-foolery allowed in study hall!" she said with a stern attitude and look.

She then walked back to the front of the class, sat down, and resumed saying her rosary.

These demonstrations of unexpected, sudden, swift, definitive punishment stuck clearly in Greg's mind for several months, but an eleven year old boy does not always think clearly, and certainly does not behave properly when goaded on by an eager class mate.

One school day still filled with the golden, morning sunshine, but with large, dark, ominous clouds on the horizon, Greg was at the first break for recess and bathroom visits.

The bathroom was a separate building from the school house. Greg was sitting in one of the toilet stalls relieving himself when all of a sudden a rotten grapefruit landed directly on his head. Looking up he saw the smiling face of his friend Bernaise, who had another rotten grapefruit in his hand. He immediately launched it, and of course it was a direct hit as he was only three feet away. This started what was forever afterwards remembered by the two them, as the great grapefruit fight.

The grapefruit tree was immediately to the right, outside the bathroom door. Thus it was very easy to replenish the rotten grape fruit ammunition from the ground under the tree. They proceeded to lob them at each other over the bathroom stall walls repeatedly, thereby quickly creating a stinking mess of broken, leaking, rotten grapefruits. They became too preoccupied with their fun activities, to notice the time slipping by. They even failed to pay attention to the loud thunder overhead, which was announcing the approaching storm. Class had resumed, and their absence was noted by the sister teaching their class. She was known as the meanest, strictest, most uncompromising sister at the entire school. She saw no humor in the rotten, smelly mess she encountered in the bathroom when she arrived. The boys were still laughing and cheering each other on, in the middle of their hilariously fun activity.

"Alright boys let's go!" she ordered, as they stood still, now interrupted and startled by her presence.

"Where to?" asked Bernaise as he wiped the dripping, rotten grapefruit juice and pulp from his face.

"Just follow me!" she barked, more sternly than ever.

They followed along, behind her black habit, as she walked in front of them. The rain now started falling heavily. There were pools of standing water forming on the ground. They followed behind the tall dark form in flowing folds of black cloth, which were rapidly becoming wet. She seemed every bit the evil specter of harsh punishment, that was coming to them, and from which there was no escape. Their fear was mounting by the seconds as they marched behind her increasingly determined steps, toward their certain punishment.

A brilliant flash of lightening temporarily blinded them. It was as if it was punctuating the fact that there was no possibility of escape. The brightness of the lightening reminded them of the white hot, searing pain in store for them. Greg's mind was now rapidly beginning to focus on his stored memories of the pain these sisters could inflict. White hot, burning, searing pain that didn't stop when the punishment ended, but the kind that kept on burning like fire for several minutes. He dreaded what was soon coming his way. He wished with all his heart and soul it was already over, but he knew all too realistically, it had not yet even begun.

They meekly followed behind her as she went into the main building's basement, and out of the rain. They then entered into a small room just large enough to accommodate the three of them. The room was crowded because of the school supplies stored there. She shut the door, and locked it with a key from her habit. Now there was definitely no escape, but then there never had been. There was a tall cylinder case standing in the corner. It contained dozens of flag pole sticks that were about three feet long. She reached into the full cylinder and chose three of them. She made a stout bundle of three sticks when she placed them together. She grabbed one end of the three stick bundle. She tested the heft of it by gently striking her other palm; it was as if she were testing it's balance, and strength. She then turned and faced the two of them, still swinging and testing it against her palm. She watched their faces as she asked,

"Who wants to be first?"

The boys looked at each other questioningly, but neither boy stepped forward. Greg was already developing tears.

"Alright then, Greg you're first! Get down on the floor." She ordered.

Bernaise watched in horror as the tall figure, dressed in all black garments, her face out lined in starched white, went to work on his best friend. Greg went to his knees, he put his face down low, close to the floor. She hunched over Greg, much as a wood chopper bends to his work. The whack, whack, whacking of the wooden poles on his back, and the shrieks of pain he emitted were the only sounds in the room. Bernaise later remembered, the room was full of the loud sounds of shrieks of pain, and the cries for mercy, and the seemingly unending, repetitive whacks. When that stack of three poles broke, she calmly chose three more, and continued her work.

Later that night Bernaise told Greg what he remembered of what he had witnessed. He said that he counted at least four different stacks of the flag pole bundles that she broke on Greg's back, and it might have been more. It seemed like it was eight to ten smacks before each of the bundles broke, and then she calmly reached for more. He said he must have lost count as his own fear began to mount. He said the shrieks of pain, and the blubbering, tearful sobs, and the sticks repeatedly breaking on his friends back, were too much to bear. And all the while, knowing, he was going to be next. Knowing there was no escape from the certain beating he would be getting; just minutes away. What made it worse and so bad he thought, was he could see exactly what was going to be happening to himself soon.

CHAPTER 7

SCHOOL ROUTINE

FOR SEVERAL MONTHS THINGS were quiet at the school, punishment wise. The days all followed the same routine, day in and day out. They went to mass every morning, and most evenings. There were always several extra special masses to attend, and there were prayer marches around their playground, all in single file, and saying the rosary. These were sometimes led by the priest, but most of the time by the head sister.

The days began at six A.M.; every one was up and dressed, the older boys helping the younger ones. Then came the marching across the street for mass at six thirty. When mass was over they marched to the dining room for breakfast. After breakfast they marched back to the study hall. Then it was time to march single file to San Antonio where classes were held. When School was over, they marched back to the dormitory. They were then allowed an hour and a half of play time, during which a treat was passed out to everyone who was not being punished. It was usually a candy bar or a piece of fruit, and was considered a high point of their day.

After play time, it was study hall time again. This was followed by dinner at the cafeteria, and then back to the study hall; for more study time or personal chores. Greg was the oldest so he had the most chores. He was assigned the tasks of making all of the younger student's beds. He shined their shoes, and cleaned and waxed the dormitory floor. This was a long room with twelve to fifteen beds on each side. Here is where the younger students slept, and where Greg had slept for two years. Now he was in a smaller room of five to six beds, in another section of the building.

In between the dormitories was the shared bathroom where every week all the students lined up to get their dose of cod liver oil, after their baths. There were no exceptions. If you did not want it the easy way, you got it the hard way. Greg observed that after once or twice, every boy chose the easy way. The three sisters never took no for an answer. No one liked watching when a reluctant boy got his the hard way. The reluctant recipient would be pinned to the floor. The arms held down at right angles to the body. The head held back and face tilted up. The nose would be pinched tight. The cod liver oil poured into the mouth. Eventually they swallowed it, and then they could get up. There was frequently some coughing, spluttering and throwing up, but they always got some of it.

It was in this larger communal bathroom that the toothpaste and toothpowder fight occurred. Greg and Bernaise were again the central figures to the confrontation, though initially there was another participant. He quickly understood this affair could come to no good, and he quietly slipped into the crowd, and was not thought of again. The fight began with Greg thinking that toothpaste would look cute on Bernaise's nose. So, he tried it on for looks. Bernaise then thought tooth powder would look even better in Greg's hair. The exchanging of paste and powder escalated until the walls, the floors, portions of the ceiling and both boys were covered with the powdered, gooey mess. When the head sister walked in they were still at it, aggressively exchanging paste and powder.

The clean up took them several hours. The repercussions and punishment required several weeks. The two of them were required to write lines. Writing lines was a usual form of punishment. They had to write one thousand times, the sentence:

"I will never participate in tooth paste and tooth powder fights in the bathroom again."

These lines had to be written by both boys. The boys had to be alone, and in separate parts of the building. They would have no free time, no special treats, no play time after school, no attendance of any events, and no special movies until the one thousand lines were written by each of them. The lines could only be written in their free time. The lines had to be legible and demonstrate good penmanship.

After three hundred lines were completed, Greg devised a way of holding two pencils together, one on top of the other, so as to write two lines at the same time. When he turned his one thousand lines in for inspection after they were completed, he remembered it took Bernaise another two weeks to complete his thousand lines. It was becoming painfully obvious to even them; that having fun, was maybe not worth having fun.

CHAPTER 8

ESCAPE AND FREEDOM

EVERY THING AT THE school was peaceful for a couple of months. The lack of excitement however created a void. The two of them eventually talked and concluded they were not having enough fun anymore. It was obvious to them something should be done about it. The two of them began to hatch a plan for their escape. They knew there were train tracks on the other side of the lake. They could hear the train's whistle at certain times when they were swimming with the rest of the boys. They knew the tracks had to be over there, somewhere. The plan was simple; they would catch a ride on a train heading south. They figured it would take them some where near Tampa, and they could manage from there. It would be a grand adventure, on the scale of Huckleberry Finn's trip down the Mississippi with the slave, Jim. There would be lots of fun and excitement.

They began to make the actual plans for their escape. Julian Morgan heard them talking about it one night, and declared he wanted to go with them. They had no objection, the more boys, the more fun and excitement to share. Their plan was simple. After breakfast the boys all walked single file back to study hall. The older boys walked first in line. The study hall room was attached to their dormitory building. The entrance to the study hall required turning a corner to the left of the dormitory building before going up the steps to enter the study hall. They would be behind the corner of the building temporarily, and thus be out of site of the sister who was always last in the line behind the younger boys.

She would not be aware of them missing until every one was inside the room. They would make their dash, all together, as soon as they turned to the left and were behind the building. They would be out of her sight. They would be in the orange groves, on the other side of their play grounds, within minutes, and would quickly disappear among the trees. They would be heading in the opposite direction from where they were really going, which were the train tracks on the other side of the lake. They thought this would help to confuse any one looking for them. On the designated morning, they were ready. When they turned the corner, they all three bolted without saying a word to any one. They ran as fast as they could, and did not slow down nor look back until they were deep among the orange grove trees. When they were well into the trees, they slowed down to a walk, to catch their breaths, and to congratulate each other on the successful escape. Finally Greg said,

"One of us should sneak back far enough to see if any one is following us."

Julian volunteered first, he said,

"Yeah, you're right, I'll do it."

He darted off back in the direction they had just come from, using the trees for cover. After several minutes he returned and said,

"No body is coming, we're in the clear, let's get moving."

They wandered along through the orange trees, eating oranges as the desire struck them. After an hour or so they came upon a large galvanized tin storage building. They climbed inside of it to hide, and rest for awhile. Once in side, they sat and talked and ate more oranges until they were full. They felt they were safe here in the metal building, as now they believed no body was coming after them. After an hour or two the temperature inside their metal shelter began to increase. The increasing heat made them think about and discuss how long they should stay in their great hide out. After talking things over and congratulating themselves again on their fine escape, and having eaten as many oranges as they could eat, they started getting bored in the increasing heat and silence of the silo. They decided it would be best to get on with their goal of getting to the rail road tracks. It would be best to get there before dark.

They left the silo, and wandered on through the orange groves, in no specific direction, because it was difficult for them to know in which direction to go. They soon came out into an open area. It was a couple of square miles in size, with a beautiful, clear, small lake in the middle of the clearing. On the shore of the lake was a large oak tree lying on the ground. It appeared to have been struck by lightening. They played and climbed and swung in the branches for a while. When they eventually got too hot and sweaty, they went for a swim in the cool waters of the lake. They stretched out to dry off on the shore of the lake, all the time enjoying their newly found freedom. After another hour or so they became bored again, and decided they better get on over to the train tracks. By now it was mid afternoon, and they realized that if they kept to the orange groves and the woods, it would take them too long to get there. It would be night time or very late when they got to the train tracks, wherever they were.

After leaving the orange groves, they came upon a dirt road which appeared to be going in the direction they thought would eventually take them in the direction of the tracks. They walked along the road, throwing rocks and joking with each other, having a great time, always enjoying the splendid freedom of doing exactly what they wanted to do. After another hour of walking they saw a dust cloud in the distance. It appeared to be getting closer to them minute by minute. Soon they could see it was definitely approaching them, and it was coming from the direction they were heading. They realized it was a car when they saw a shiny reflection coming out of the dust cloud. They got off the road immediately, and hid behind the trees as fast as they could. As the car got closer they could tell it was a police car, first from the markings and then from the bubble of lights on the top. The car stopped on the road beside their trees. The officer stepped out of the car and looked around for a second or two. He walked over to where they were hiding behind the trees. When he got close enough he said, "You boys doing O.K?"

They stepped out from behind the trees, and looked at him in bewilderment and disappointment, and he added, "Yeah, you are, but I think you better come with me."

When they arrived back at the convent, the day had turned into darkness. They were taken straight to the head sisters office. When they entered her office they were faced not only by the head sister, but also by all six of their parents. It was not a pleasant meeting for them. The parents displayed relief on their faces at first, but the anger and disappointment followed quickly enough.

By the time the meeting was over, the boys had all apologized. They all said they were sorry to have caused so much trouble. To every one's surprise, even their own, they declared to a boy they really did not want to be kicked out of the school. They just wanted to have some fun. They promised they would be good, and not cause any more problems in the future. They truly realized their adventure had caused a lot of unnecessary trouble, for the school, their parents, the police and themselves.

CHAPTER 9

CONVERSION

AFTER RETURNING TO THE school, Greg could see that what he had done for fun had caused very much trouble for a large number of people. He realized that he was feeling guilty for what he had done. This realization was a major turning point in Greg's life. He found to his amazement, he felt truly sorry for what he had done. As the weeks went by, he developed a surprising and increasing desire to become more religious. He understood and now believed that by becoming a catholic he could best please God, and he now wanted to do that above all else. He had recently become more intimately acquainted with hell, and he was convinced he did not want to go there. The rest of the year he caused no more problems. He became a model student. He declared to every one he wanted to become a catholic. He got his own prayer book, The Catholic Missal, and he tried to read it when he felt the call. He carried it to mass every morning and evening. He started wearing a scapular. The scapular was made from a pair of pieces of special cloth, that were connected by two strings the size of shoe laces. He wore it with one cloth in front and one cloth in back. He wore his scapular at all times, because it was taught to him, that if he died while wearing it, he would be assured of going to heaven. He now knew he wanted to go to heaven. The thought of sitting in a burning fire for eternity was not something he wanted. The more he tried to think about eternity, and how long that was, the more convinced he was he did not want to be sitting in a big fiery inferno for eternity. Even a small flame from a match burned his finger more than he could tolerate. How could he or anybody else possibly tolerate huge fires burning him all over his body, and for eternity? It was beyond his comprehension. Every time he had an impulse of doing something bad, the thought of those fires licking at him, and being all around him, and burning his entire body, for eternity, stopped him. These type of thoughts soon made him think of doing good things only. He was determined to be only a good boy from that time on. When the sixth grade was coming to an end, he was constantly asking the sisters when he could become a catholic. The head sister, knowing his family were not Catholics, convinced him he should wait until he returned to public schools and resume living with his family. If after a sufficient period of time, his family and he were still in agreement, then he could be confirmed a catholic.

He was fine with that plan, because now there was no hurry. He knew he was going to be good from now on, and for the rest of his life. He was sure of that. He also had his scapular to wear now, so he was safe from going to hell and all those fires. He wanted to be perfect for his God. It now made him feel better than when he was doing bad things against God.

CHAPTER 10

SUMMER IN GEORGIA

When Catholic boarding school was over that year, he was sent to Georgia for the summer to work in the tobacco fields with his fathers's relatives. He was eleven years old. In three months he would be twelve. This was his third summer of working in the tobacco fields for his Georgia relatives. He missed the last year because of being in California. When he was in Georgia he always lived with his Great Aunt Lou. She was his grandmother's sister. She looked like his grandmother, and reminded him of her. Her house was at the end of a dirt lane road. With the exception of her son's house, it was the only house with in several miles. Her son lived a quarter of a mile away, closer to the highway. He had a wife and a son who was a year younger than Greg. His name was Jeryl. Later that summer Greg would learn that Jeryl was very close to one of his younger female cousins. This fact alone put Daryl on a different level from his other cousins in Greg's mind. He had never known any one who could get along with girls like Jeryl could. Some how he knew how to talk with girls, and they all seemed to like him immediately. If they all went swimming after work was done, the girls were always hanging around with Jeryl. They were always laughing and joking with him, to the exclusion of the other boys. In Greg's view this ability to have all the girls like him, was definitely something Greg wanted to have for himself. It was a complete mystery to Greg, this ability of Jeryl to get along so well with the opposite sex.

Aunt Lou was a widow. In spite of her advanced age she managed the house, the pigs, the mules, the cows, the chickens, and all the kids who stayed with her, all by herself. It was going to be the ultimate summer for Greg. He was looking forward to living like Tom Sawyer and Huckleberry Finn. He would get to be barefoot all summer long. He loved being at Aunt Lou's house. There was no running water at the house. There was no in door plumbing, and no electricity. She was an observing and practicing Hard Shell Baptist, and she followed all the rules, except for her secret snuff, which she offered no excuses for, to anybody. Greg learned that any type of modern conveniences was not allowed by her church. Their water came from a well under the house, it was drawn up by a hand pump on the back porch, and then was carried in to the house in pails. All of the cooking was done on a wood fired stove. The wood for the stove was wood that Greg and his cousins cut and stacked when they were with her. There were dozens of chickens running around loose in the all dirt yard. There were several large pigs and piglets for him to slop morning and night. There were two cows to milk, and two mules to care for. Their vegetables came from the fields behind the house. They picked their vegetables by hand, and they chose daily what they wanted to eat for that day. The fresh eggs were collected from the laying chickens in the hen house. There was a smoke house immediately behind the main house. It was filled with different meats from the annuals laughter of animals. The meat was slowly smoked over many days by Aunt Lou and her son, and kept there in the smoke house. Greg helped with all the chores, and he enjoyed a chew of delicious smoked ham from time to time with his other cousins.

There was a large wood fired iron cauldron in the shed next to the smoke house. It was here they made their own syrup from their sugar cane patch. This making of the cane syrup was one of Greg's favorite activities during the summer. As the sugar cane boiled down, crystals of pure cane sugar formed on the wide lip of the cauldron. The boys were allowed to scrape the hot sugar crystals off of the edge of the boiling sugarcane juices. They were able to do this with long flat strips of sugar cane peelings that came from the cane stalks they cut up. They cut the cane in proper lengths so they would fit into the cauldron of boiling syrup. It was like having fresh candy, hot off the pan.

Greg always had a slight apprehension when ever he was alone in the cauldron shed or even with one of his cousins. It was well known fact, that Uncle Dan, Aunt Lou's husband when he was alive, had encountered a panther in the shed one night while he was going to the outhouse. The outhouse was on the other side of the fence which enclosed the shed. Uncle Dan had simply grabbed up an axe, cleaved the panther in the head, and killed it with several more blows. Greg did not like using the outhouse when it was dark, so he some time went out in the front yard when he had to pee at night, instead of using the slop jar under the bed. Greg loved his summers in Georgia. He never wore shoes the entire summer. All the boys went barefoot everywhere, even when they went in to town. They used to go in to town on Sundays to sell their boiled peanuts. They pulled their own peanuts out of the ground, and boiled them in large steaming pots. They put them into paper sacks, and sold them in Patterson, which was several miles south of where they lived. Greg always imagined he was living like Tom Sawyer and Huckleberry Finn during the summers he spent in Georgia. It was wonderful to him. After work was finished for the day, they all went to the favorite swimming hole in the river that was near by.

He wore his scapular from the catholic boarding school every where, all of the time, even when they went swimming in the river after work was done for the day. He did everything possible to be as good a boy as he could be. He did not want to take a chance on dying without having his scapular around his neck. Those thoughts of sitting around in hell, with those burning flames licking away at him, for all of eternity, were still very fresh and vivid in his memory.

That summer he learned from his older cousins about self stimulation.

He did wonder at times if God thought it was all right for him to experience pleasure from the activity. He also wondered if

God kept boys out of heaven because of it. Just in case, he made sure to keep his scapular on at all time. That seemed like such an easy insurance policy, because he was not sure what God's attitude might be.

This summer, which was his last, he was offered to ride the mules that pulled the tobacco sleds. He loved riding the mules. When he was in California the last summer, he rode a broom stick with a rope tied to one end for the bridal, and pretended it was a real horse. He loved the feeling of riding horses, even broom stick horses. He sat proudly on the mule, and guided the mule up and down the rows of the tobacco plants, smiling all the time. He liked this job much more than his other jobs in previous years. In the past he had helped do all of the other jobs involved in getting the tobacco from the plants, in the field, to the market.

The tobacco plants were grown in long straight rows, in huge fields. This year his job was to guide the mule, who pulled a long sled behind it, up and down the rows of tobacco plants. The "pickers" pulled the leaves off of the plants and put them in the sled. When the sled was full, Greg guided the mule from the fields to the tobacco barns. Here, in front of the barn, the green leaves were unloaded from the sled, and placed on a long bench. That was where the "handers" sat to pass the leaves. The leaves were handed to the "stringer". The "stringer's" job was to take a handful of the tobacco leaves from the "handers." There were three or four leaves to a hand-full, and the stringer's job was to string them on to a stick. The stick was five feet long. The "stringer" would secure a stout string to one end of the stick. The "handers" would then pass the hand-full of leaves to the "stringer", who would secure the leaves to the stick by a quick double loop of the string. The group of leaves would then be strung continuously and were alternated between the right and left sides of the stick, where they hung securely as long as they were kept right side up. When the stick was filled to the other end, the string was tied off. The stick with the green leaves hanging down, would then be ready to be hung on the rafters inside the barns, later in the day. The rafters were the exact size to accommodate the tobacco laden sticks. When all of the picking, handing, and stringing work was done for the day, it was time to hang the tobacco sticks inside the barn. In the barn, the rafters reached up, two or three stories high. It would take four or five persons stationed at different levels on the rafters, to pass the tobacco, from person to person, up to the top most rafters. They would fill the barn from top to bottom. When the barn was full, it was ready to be "fired". The "firing" would take place at another time from loading the tobacco in to the barn. The summers work was to fill one barn, after another, until all of the tobacco fields were empty.

All of his relatives worked together. The families helping each other harvest the different fields. Before the picking of the mature tobacco leaves, the plants had to be, "wormed and suckered." To accomplish the worming process, someone had to walk up and down the rows, and pull off the green worms, which were some times two or three inches long, and as fat as a man's finger. They clung tenaciously to the tobacco plants, and you had to kill them, so they could not get back on the plants. Greg did not like this part of the job. He had to do it with bare fingers, and he disliked the sensation of squishing then with his fingers, and getting their juices on his hands. Another step was to "sucker" the tobacco plants. This had to be done periodically. This was a similar process to the worming, in that it required removing the sucker leaves by hand. These were not going to become good tobacco leaves, and they stole nutrition from the good leaves. The worming and removing of the "sucker leaves" was all done by firm hands, and good eyes. The next step, when the leaves were mature and ready, was to pick the tobacco leaves, and stack them in the sleds drawn by the mule.

The firing of the barns was another one of Greg's favorites. This required some one to stay at the barn, all night, to keep the wood fires going continuously for several days, until the tobacco was cured. This was the job all of the boys loved most. Here they fed long planks of cut wood into the furnaces, which were built in to the barns, but attached to the outside, so the firing could be done without opening the doors. They got to sleep at the barns all night, keeping the fires going until the tobacco was cured. They got to be alone, without adult supervision much of the time. There was always a lot of playing around, and joking with each other during those nights. Sometimes they would try a plug of chewing tobacco, or take a puff off of a cigarette or a cigar. Greg always got a little dizzy, and sometimes nauseated from the chewing tobacco, but he would never think of not participating in the ritual with the other boys. It was not unusual for certain of the boys to sometimes engage in a marathon story telling event before the night was over, thus adding one more enjoyable dimension to the evenings activities. Greg loved riding the mules the most of all the different jobs. All he had to do was sit on the mules, and guide them from the fields to the barns where the" handers" were waiting for the next load of tobacco. When Greg was a "hander, he frequently had black widow spiders, that clung to the tobacco leaves, climbing over his lap and thighs. Every one did, but they simply brushed them off. Greg was surprised to never hear of a "hander" getting bitten by the black widow spiders, because there were so many of them, every where, all the time. Every one had heard the story about Uncle Joe. He had been bitten on the rear end while using the outhouse, and almost died from it.

He did have one bad experience during the summer. It happened with a mule he was riding about mid summer. He had just dropped off a load of tobacco leaves, and was heading back to the field for another load. As the mule approached the turn to the left, which would take them back to the field, he pulled on the left rein, like he had always done. The mule kept walking straight. When it got to the next row it turned to the right, and followed that road. Greg was pulling on the reins, with all his strength, shouting commands, and pleading with the mule to stop. Nothing Greg did had any effect on the mule. It just kept on walking, pulling the empty sled behind it. The next road was to the left, and it turned and followed that road. Greg realized with horror, there was nothing he could do to make the mule change directions. The next road turned right, and led to another empty and unattended tobacco barn. When they arrived at the front of that barn, the mule stopped, and stood there, calmly ignoring Greg's imploring commands and pleadings.

Greg climbed off of the mule's back, and jumped to the ground. He could not make the mule move from where it stopped. He started crying in frustration. The tears were streaming down his face as he cried. He was walking around the mule, crying and cursing the mule when he saw someone walk from behind the barn. As the man approached, Greg recognized him, he was an old black man. All the kids called him Uncle Remus, because he looked like Uncle Remus. As he approached, he smiled and asked Greg,

"What's going on here? Come on now child. Stop that crying, and tell ole Uncle Remus what's going on here?" When Greg was finally able to stop crying, and get control of himself, he said,

"This dumb old mule won't listen to me. He just goes where he wants to go. I pull on the reins and he won't pay me no mind." He managed to say between sobs.

Uncle Remus was a very old man. He had a full white beard, and a very black face. When he smiled, Greg could see only a few whitish snags of front teeth. He wore old, faded blue coveralls. His shirt was very thin and the sleeves had worn out holes at the elbows. He smiled, kindly at Greg and said,

"Well now, les see what we can do here to make this mule listen to you."

He walked around in front of the mule. He put his face inches away from the mule's nose, he then looked him right in the eyes. He grabbed the halter in both hands and shook it gently, and said,

"Now listen here mule, you pay attention to this here boy, and do what he say.", He shook the halter gently, again, as he continued looking the mule right in the eyes. Then he turned to Greg and said,

"I think he do what you say now. You can stop crying now child. Let's get you back up on that mule, and get him moving on down that road yonder there, and get him back to work."

Greg let Uncle Remus put him back up on the mule. Then Uncle Remus took hold of the halter and led the mule back in the direction from which he had come. After he walked about five minutes, he let go of the halter, and said,

"He be O.K. now, You can get him on back to work."

From that time on, the mule always did what Greg asked him to do. Greg never did understand completely what happened that day.

He chose to believe however, that it was God who had sent Uncle Remus to help him when he needed it most. Maybe it was God himself pretending to be Uncle Remus. Or maybe Uncle Remus was just a messenger from God. How could he know, but he never told any one about Uncle Remus, the stubborn mule, or about how much he had cried that day.

CHAPTER 11

END OF SUMMER

AT THE END OF the tobacco season, when all the fields had been picked, and the tobacco fired, it was time to unstring the tobacco sticks They put the tobacco leaves in to large sheets of croaker sack material, and tied the bundles at the top. These bundles were about six feet across and three feet high. They were perfect to climb on and play, and sometime to sleep on. These bundles were taken to the city of Blackshear, twenty miles south. This was where the tobacco auctions were held every year. The auction event was one of the best times of the summer for the boys. It was a circus like atmosphere, with all the busy crowds and colorful activity. It was a time when it seemed every one came to town to participate in the fun. For the boys the auctions were spectacles to behold; days filled with crowds of people, continuous auctioning of the tobacco, and many food and drink stands. The auctioneers spoke so fast that only the buyers could understand what was being said and what was happening. The boys roamed freely about the huge auction halls, taking in all the sights, sounds, smells and ambiance. Jeryl was always there it seemed to Greg, with his entourage of young girls always following him around, laughing and giggling among them selves. Greg was envious of how popular Jeryl was with all the girls, but so far he could not understand why he was like a magnet for them.

Greg really liked this part of his summers in Georgia, but he also knew that this activity signaled the end of his tobacco season for the year. He knew that now that the summer was over, he would be returning to Tampa. He would be going to a new school, in a completely different area of the city. He would not know anyone. He would have to start wearing shoes again. He was not looking forward to returning to Tampa.

PART 2

CHAPTER 12

MEETING SKIPPER

WHEN THE SUMMER ACTIVITIES were over, he rode the train back to Tampa. His stepfather met him at the station with the news that his mother was in the hospital, she was recovering from a surgical procedure and had developed some sort of complication. Greg had to live with his stepfather for a week or so; during which time they did not become any closer. By the time his mother got out of the hospital, it was time to begin the seventh grade at Memorial Junior High school. That was the year he met Skipper.

When Greg asked if he could join a Boy Scout troop his mother readily agreed. She knew there was one in the Elks building next door to the beauty shop where she worked. They found out that the this troop was sponsored by the Elks Club. They met every Wednesday night at six P.M. The very next Wednesday night, Greg was the first one of the boys to be at the door. He was eager to meet the other scouts. Soon they began to arrive, and he introduced himself to every one. When the scout master arrived, they began the meeting. Greg liked the scout master right away. He was as tall as his father, which meant he was over six feet. He reminded Greg of the handsome actor who played superman in the movies. He had the same shaped face. His hair was dark brown and was cut short all over and it lay close to his skull. He had a warm friendly smile, and he was always smiling. He had dark brown eyes. They seemed to twinkle when he smiled. He was slightly chubby around the middle, so he did not look like superman in that regard.

He had been the troop master for the past year and a half. He was a major in the air force, and he was now stationed at MacDill Air Force Base. He was not a pilot. His dark brown eyes were very kind and comforting when he looked at you. All of the scouts seemed to like him very much. The meeting began with the introduction of the Elk Club member who was assigned to be the representative to the scout troop. He made some general remarks about how proud the Elks organization was to sponsor the scout troop in they're building. He said he felt very confident that under the leadership of this scout master, the troop was certain to produce many fine Life and Eagle Scouts, and that the troop would certainly train many youths to develop in to responsible citizens by following the guidelines of the Boy Scouts of America. He went on to say that, as scouts, they should all strive for better character development, and self reliance, through participation in the wide range of activities that were available to them with this particular troop. The Elk Club was very proud to be able to provide a room for the scouts to meet and learn. Finally, he said we should all be very happy and proud to have a major in the air force, who was willing to donate his time to help our youths achieve their goals of becoming the very best of the Boy scouts of America. After the Elk representative was applauded by the scouts, he left the room.

The scout master then stood in front of the troop and said, "My name is Skipper, you can call me Skip, or you can call me Skipper. I answer to both. I am now, and I will be your scout master. As usual we will begin the meeting with the scout oath and the scout law. Then we will have every one tell what they did to honor the scout slogan this week. So, let's begin troop".

The Group stood and all together recited the oath.

"On my honor I will do my best
to do my duty to God and my country
and to obey the scout law
to help other people at all times
to keep myself physically strong
mentally awake and morally straight."

"Very good troop, now let's all repeat the scout law." Skipper said.

In unison they all said.

"A scout is trustworthy, loyal, helpful, friendly, courteous, kind, obedient, cheerful, thrifty, brave, clean and reverent."

"All right, how many scouts do we have tonight who would like to share with the troop their effort to fulfill the scout slogan, which is what, Tommy?" Tommy stood and said,

"Do A Good Turn Daily." Then he sat down.

With this request only three of the scouts raised their hands.

"O.K., we will hear them in a minute. First will be Joe, then Peter, and then Matthew. Before we hear about the good turns, we have a new candidate for membership in our troop tonight. Would you please stand, introduce yourself, and tell us something about you, and then tell us what your goals may be." Greg now flushed with embarrassment; he was not use to speaking in front of a crowd. He forced himself to stand and with shaky knees and a weak voice, said,

"My name is Greg Saunders. I'm twelve years old. I'm new to town. I am in the seventh grade at Memorial Junior High school. I want to be a scout because, I have heard they are always the best a boy can be. I know that scouts in general have as their goal to make boys more self reliant through out door activities, like camping, hiking and water sports. I like all of those things. So I believe I will fit right in, and I will make a good scout"

"It sounds like you may have been reading something about the Boy Scouts, Greg." Skipper said with a wide grin. This statement coming from Skipper, the scout master, made Greg more relaxed, and he said, "Yes. I have been reading, because I want to be a good scout, and I think I'm ready to be a scout. I know that being prepared is an important part of being a scout". Greg felt himself flushing again. Then Skipper said,

"It never hurts to be prepared, isn't that right troop? The troop responded by saying out loud, like a chant,

"Be Prepared"

"Tonight it is especially important for us to be on time at the Y.M.C.A. Pool. They have it scheduled for another function, just as soon as our time is up. So every one get together with your work group for tonight, and start on the merit badges you want to achieve. By now you all know who you are meeting with. I will be circulating around to meet with each group, and help out with any specific questions or problems. Greg, you start tonight with the tenderfoot group. That is the usual place for beginners.

Now let's hear from our three scouts who did a good deed today. Joe, you're first." Skipper said.

"I helped my next door neighbor. She is an older woman. She locked herself out of the house. I climbed in through the bathroom window, and unlocked the door for her. She would not have been able to squeeze through the small window." Joe said.

"Very good, Joe. Your turn Peter." said Skipper.

"I helped my homeroom teacher carry in some large boxes from her car this morning. She would have had to make several trips, and it was a long way from her car." said Peter.

"That definitely qualifies as a good turn Peter. Now it's your turn Matt.", said Skipper.

"I helped an old man get up off the ground. He tripped on the curb when he tried to cross the street. I helped him get up, and across the street. I think he twisted his ankle, because he was limping after I got him up from the fall." said Matthew.

"Good for all three of you. Thank you for sharing with us." said Skipper.

Greg was happy to be at the meeting, it felt good to begin the process of becoming a scout. The Tenderfoots group consisted of the most recent members. They focused on the basics of being a scout. They learned about the history of the organization, the goals, the scout methods and their values. Greg asked the boy next to him who had just shared his good turn story.

"What's this about swimming tonight?" asked Greg.

"After the meeting is over, every one in the troop goes swimming at the Y. We do it after every meeting. It's great fun, and it's free to us as scouts. Some of us play tag, others just swim." said Matthew.

Greg felt an unhappy expression begin to develop on his face and he said

"It sounds like a lot of fun, but I didn't bring a bathing suit with me tonight." Greg said.

"No problem, we don't wear swim suits at the Y.M.C.A. pool, no body does." Matthew said.

"Really?" said Greg with a big smile." That's good. Then, I am prepared. Maybe I will make a good scout."

"Hey! That's a good one Greg. You're prepared, because you don't have a bathing suit." said Matt, with a laugh.

"Your name is Mathew?" Greg asked.

"Matt, just Call me Matt, nice to meet you"

"Yes. I'm really happy to meet you too Matt. I hope you and me can become good friends, Greg said.

"I'm certain we can." said Matt.

Later, at the pool, in the basement of the Y.M.C.A. building; two blocks from the Elks building, the boys hurriedly undressed and raced to the showers. They then all went to the pool side where they stood around naked, waiting for the word from their scout master to begin play. When Skipper arrived, Greg noticed he was the only one who remained fully clothed. He always stayed clothed while the boys swam, he learned. When he gave the word, they all jumped in and began playing. Initially they all swam back and forth long ways in the pool. Soon, the personal splashing began. Eventually the tag game started. One side of the pool was a wall of the building. There was a narrow ledge, the boys could stand on, against the wall. It made a tag safe place on which to stand while playing, because it was hard to reach anyone on the ledge. If the "IT" person approached from the water one could easily move right or left; or they could leap over them and scramble quickly up the other side of the pool. If they approached on the ledge, it was possible to escape in the other direction. Greg found he could stay ahead of almost any pursuer. He discovered that if you were a fast enough swimmer, it was hard for any one to catch you. He was fast enough, because he was not caught that night. He felt a sense of pride in himself for his swimming skills. He thought that Skipper seemed to be looking in his direction a lot, maybe Skipper had also noted his swimming skills.

Running on the slippery, wet surfaces was not allowed, but many times in the heat of pursuit, or escape, the rules were not followed. On Greg's first night no one was hurt, but he could see many possibilities for injuries to occur. Later that night, lying in his bed at home, he felt very sure he was going to enjoy being in the scouts. The scouts were always learning new and different things for their merit badges. Greg had already discovered within himself how much he liked learning about new and different things.

CHAPTER 13

FITTING IN

As the weeks and months passed, Greg increasingly felt like he was enjoying himself and having a good year. He was in a great scout troop. School was going well. He met several new friends that he liked. He also liked his home room teacher. She was a tall woman, middle age with dark black hair. She was a person whose demeanor commanded respect from the class in a natural and easy way. Her style of teaching was unhurried and relaxed, and because of this, the majority of the students behaved in her classes. This was true even for some of the more undisciplined boys who, almost always, caused trouble in some of the other class rooms. One of Greg's class mates who sat next to him, had a way of whistling through his front teeth. He sounded like a chirping bird. He could do this without any one in the room knowing who was doing the bird whistling. He didn't move his lips, so unless you were sitting next to him, you could not discern who was making the whistling sounds. Greg practiced the technique until he was almost as good as his friend. Occasionally he would use his anonymous whistling technique on teachers he did not like, or if he thought they were unfair, to another class mate. He never considered doing it in his home room classes, because he respected and liked his teacher too much. Greg met a bigger boy in his physical education class, who convinced him he should try out for the foot ball team. His name was Bill. He was very mature for his age. Bill was going to try out for a lineman position, either guard or tackle, when the football season began. Greg liked Bill a lot from the very beginning, so he thought he would try playing football too. Greg knew he was still small in stature for football, but he had heard of boys his size who had made the team in previous years. So he had hopes it would work out. One of the things Greg liked about Bill was that he was the smartest boy in the school. He maintained a straight "A" average grade level. Another thing he really liked about Bill was that he was always talking about girls and their special attribute, and even though Greg had no experience with girls yet himself, he thought that the more he knew now, the better it would be for him later. So he enjoyed hanging out as much as he could with Bill because he was already comfortable around girls, and he loved talking about them and all the things boys secretly discuss; sometimes describing in graphic detail some of his exploits. From what he said, he was getting all the girl company he wanted, and all that that implied. Greg soon learned that Bill was one of those guys who the girls loved to be with. He reminded Greg of his cousin Jeryl in Georgia. He always had girls hanging around him, and wanting to be with him, just like Bill. What ever they had that the girls liked, he wanted some of it, but he had no idea what it was. Greg found himself looking at the girls more and more. He also felt stronger yearnings than for just watching them, and he began anticipating what it would be like to have this one or that one for a friend. He realized that he had to grow up more, but he did know and believe that eventually his turn would come. As far as he was concerned, it couldn't come soon enough, but for now he listened and learned from experienced people like Bill, who was already doing what he wanted to be doing with girls.

CHAPTER 14

ASKED TO THE RANCH

When Greg was asked by Skipper to go to the ranch for the week end, for the first time, he was thrilled and excited. Over the past few months he had been told, by some of the other boys in the troop how much fun it was at the ranch. There were so many things to see and to do they said. He was so excited, he could hardly sleep the night before he was to go. The next morning he was picked up by Skipper and three other boys. He knew them all from the scout troop. Greg later learned that of the three boys; Joe was the oldest, he had been going to the ranch for the past year and a half. Tommy was the next oldest. He had been going for the past nine months. Matt was Greg's age. Greg knew Matt from the first night in the scouts. He had been going to the ranch for the past four months. Joe was four years older than Greg, and Tommy was a year older. Tommy had already told Greg about the private lake, that was deep in the cypress swamp, in front of the house. He said he caught perch, bream, bass, trout, and catfish every time he went fishing there. Greg was ready and eager to catch some fish himself. At seven thirty, the car stopped in front of the house. It was a light blue Henry J. Coupe. Tommy and Matt were in the back seat. Joe was in the front, in the passenger's seat. Skipper was driving. Greg's mother and stepfather had already left for work, so Greg grabbed his bag, locked the front door, and ran for the car.

"You can ride in the back Greg. Put your bag in the trunk." said Joe.

When Greg was in his seat, Skipper said,

"Are you ready for some breakfast? We stop at our favorite place in Sulfur Springs on the way out of town?"

"Oh, sure I'm hungry. What do you all usually like to eat?" Greg said.

"Let's see what's on the menu." Skipper said. They drove the half block to Nebraska Avenue, and turned right. The boys all looked at Greg, and smiled, they seemed genuinely sincere, and happy he was there. Greg felt like he was warmly welcomed aboard.

They drove north on Nebraska Avenue. When they passed over the Hillsborough River bridge they drove past the large swimming pool complex on the left hand side. This pool and its beach was a very special place for Greg. When he was much younger, his father and mother brought him here for family outings. It was his favorite place to swim in all of Tampa. Greg had spent most of his life swimming at this particular pool. The only times he missed was while in boarding school and when in California. It picked up again the year his mother worked at the beauty shop across the street. It was a large circular pool with deep vertical concrete walls. In the middle, was a huge fresh water spring. He remembered how much fun it was to be swept over the edge of the pool, and be rapidly rushed down the water slide to the lower level pool. The water slide was where the overflow of the upper pool escaped to the lower level.

Once on the lower level pool, you were swept down stream by the current. There was a long beach of fine white sand, which was in front of the bath house. The beach was on the right hand side of the swimming area as you were swept down stream by the current. Further down stream it flowed in to the Hillsborough River. This was where he had seen manatees swimming on the other side of a thick wire barricade. The barricade separated the swimming area from the main river. It was not the most attractive area of the complex to Greg. Greg suddenly remembered being in the middle of the main pool, he remembered it clearly now. He envisioned seeing himself diving, diving, down deep, trying to see the source of the spring, and where the flowing waters came from; only to be swept back upward again by the tremendous flow of fresh water. These memories then made him think of the time he had tumbled backwards, from the top of the ten foot diving board, on to the concrete surface at the base of the ladder. He had landed flat on his back, in a shallow pool of water at the base of the ladder. He smiled as he remembered how, at the time it happened, he thought he must be dying. He could not take a breath of air into his lungs for several minutes, because all the air had been knocked out of him. He then remembered how lucky he was not to have been killed by the fall, and how incredulous his mother was when he told her about it. The pool was a very special place for him.

They drove on north for another mile, and then pulled into a parking space in front of a small restaurant on the right hand side of the street. It was a place Greg had walked by many times, but had never been in because his family did not dine out very much. As they entered the restaurant, with Skipper coming in last, there was an exuberance of greetings by the staff and the owner. Their group seemed to be well known by the staff and some of the patrons. When the greetings were over, they sat down to look at the menus.

"Do you like eggs Greg?" Skipper asked.

"Sure." Greg answered.

"Do you like steak?" he asked.

"Oh yeah!" Greg said, enthusiastically.

"Then unless any one wants something else, we will take five of the steak and egg specials." Skipper said to the waitress.

"Coffee for every body?" she asked.

"I prefer hot chocolate." Tommy said.

By the time the food arrived Greg was becoming hungrier. It was a big juicy steak with two eggs, sunny side up. There was barely enough room for the hash brown potatoes. The talking among them ceased as they ate their breakfasts. Greg was surprised and impressed by the sumptuous breakfast. He was not used to such a special treat like this for breakfast, but it seemed obvious to him now, the other boys were. While they were finishing the coffee, toast and jelly, Skipper said.

"We find that we do better with a full stomach, before we get to the ranch, then we can get right on with our days activities. That way Mrs. Parker doesn't have to make breakfast for us."

After breakfast was over they drove northon U.S 41, for half an hour. Greg noticed that Tommy was sitting between Skipper's legs, steering the car. Greg found this was a common routine the boys all followed on the drive to the ranch. The boys liked to take advantage of learning to drive at any opportunity they had, because they sometimes got to drive an old ford truck, which was kept on the ranch property. When they came to state road 52, they turned left. They were now heading west toward the Gulf of Mexico. Greg was following their progress on the map. When they were almost half way to U.S. 19 they turned left onto a dirt road heading south.

CHAPTER 15

THE RANCH

GREG COULD THEN SEE the house, straight ahead, about a third of a mile away. As they drove under the pole and plank archway into the yard, he could see a small light tan dog with large floppy ears running toward them, and begin to circle the car. There were several loose chickens milling around in the yard. He immediately thought of Georgia and Aunt Lou's chickens. He saw a one armed man, and a woman, come out of the door at the back of the house. The man's left arm was missing above the elbow. The couple approached when the car stopped. Greg could see that she was much older than Skipper. She had mostly grey hair that was cut short just below the ears. She wore bifocal glasses. She had on a simple dress with a large white apron with which she was drying her hands. The one armed man was bald on top but he had a thick fringe of salt and pepper colored hair. He was of medium build, but had compact knotty muscles in his right arm. When the greetings ended, Skipper introduced Greg to Mrs. Parker, and her husband Lindsey. Tommy and Matt were already playing with the dog, causing the loose chickens to scatter, running and flying in different directions. Joe had already started unloading the car. He was putting their things in to a wooden wheel barrow to be transported in to the house.

"No, we won't be needing anything to eat right now. We had a big breakfast before leaving town." Skipper said to Mrs. Parker.

"Then let' s go in the house, and show Greg around." Mrs. Parker said.

They entered the house through the back door. Once inside Mrs. Parker explained the lay out of the house. "On the left here, by the back door, is our pantry. On the right you can see the stove and the sink next to it. Straight on over to the right is our eating table with the benches on each side. If we need more seating, the table expands out this way and we use extra chairs. We go in to the living room this way."The door to the front of the house was in the middle of the living room. It opened to a covered wide porch that was almost as big as the living room. It was as long as the house. Opposite the front door was the back side of the living room. There was a couch and two chairs against the wall, facing the front of the house; there were two windows which looked out to the back yard.

"Straight on that way is the bathroom, it is in the middle of the two bedrooms. The bedroom on the right is where all you boys and Skipper sleep, and to the left is where Lindsey and I sleep. It's our private room and we like to keep it that way. So you boys stay out." She said with a knowing smile.

When Greg went in to the boys bedroom, he saw a queen sized bed. It was in the middle of the room with the head against the far wall. There were two single cots against the wall at the foot of the bed. He learned that there was another fold up cot in the closet if needed. There were two windows in the room. One was by the head of the big bed and the other by the head of the cot next to the front of the house.

"Greg, why don't you go outside and get Matt and Tommy to show you around. I've got some business to go over with the Parkers." said Skipper.

The boys showed him the chicken coop and the pen, and they explained how it was their responsibility when at the ranch, to put the chickens inside at night. They showed him the work shop behind the back of the house where the tools were kept. There was a model A Ford pick up truck with wooden rails around the flat bed of the truck. It was kept under the cover of the shed attached to the shop.

"Can you drive that truck, Greg?"Tommy asked.

"Not yet, but I bet it won't take me long, once I start." said Greg.

"Where is this lake you been telling me about?" Greg asked.

"Our lake's in the middle of that cypress swamp, in front of the house. We'll go down and go fishing in a little while. We can go almost any time we want. We can always count on catching enough fish for our dinner. We have to tell some adult when we go to the lake. They have to know where to look for us, if we are late getting back. When we go to the lake, you will want to go barefoot, or wear some type of water shoes that can get wet. Most of the time the boards we walk on are partially under water, particularly if it's been raining very much. Let's go get us some worms right now, so we can be ready." Tommy said.

They walked down to the higher ground at the edge of the swamp. With in ten minutes they found a suitable moist place, and soon dug up a whole can of juicy, fat, plump earth worms. They filled the can with the worms and the moist, dark, rich earth. They put in enough dirt to keep the worms completely covered. They asked Joe if he wanted to go fishing with them. He said he wanted to go, but needed to finish working on his merit badge project, and would be using the shop and the tools while they were gone. He wished them luck and said he would help them clean the catch, when they got back. He said he recently learned a new way of skinning catfish. He just learned it, and he wanted to share the technique with them.

"Will you tell the adults that three of us are down at the lake? You can also tell them we're going to catch dinner for every one." Tommy said.

"You had better catch something, or one of you will have to kill a chicken for dinner." Joe said smiling.

"I know how to ring a chicken's neck. I used to do it in Georgia." said Greg.

He remembered having to catch them, and wring their necks, when he was living with his Aunt Lou. He wanted to show off to the other boys that he could do it, even though he did not enjoy it. He had never liked doing it, but he wanted to show them he could help out, him being the newest boy at the ranch. He always felt sorry for which ever chicken he had to choose, as he grabbed it by the head, and started spinning and wrenching the chicken's body clock wise around his hand.

After he had done it, he did not like watching them flopping around on the ground. They would flop, hop and spin in all different directions, until all movement finally ceased. That was one part of the chores he liked the least. He didn't even like killing the tobacco plant worms, much less chickens.

CHAPTER 16

THE LAKE

EACH OF THE THREE boys chose a cane pole with hooks, corks, lines and sinkers already prepared. They took off their shoes on the front porch, and started walking barefoot down hill toward the cypress swamp in front of the house. This immediately reminded Greg of his summers in Georgia. He loved being barefoot. He always felt better whenever his bare feet were touching the ground. The trees of the swamp were about fifty yards from the back gate. Greg saw there was a noticeable grade gradually going down hill, as they walked away from the house. They entered the swamp and walked another fifty yards before they were walking in shallow water. Greg could see that the trail continued going slightly down hill. The trail they followed was made of flat cut cedar boards. They were laid out end to end. Greg could see the trail ahead of them snaking and twisting it's way through the swamp. Overhead the trail was covered by a thick canopy of leafy branches and hanging vines that blocked out the sun; except for an occasional shaft of sun beam light, which illuminated small patches of ground and water as it pierced the canopy. The boards were eight to twelve inches wide; two or three of the boards were placed side by side. They were just wide enough to create a narrow platform, on which to balance and walk. There were many different lengths of boards, so each board spanned a distance of it's own length, going from log to log, or on top of stumps of cypress trees, that had bee cut when the path was originally cleared. Sometime in the long past, It had been cleared with axes and saws. Greg found he had to have good balance not to fall off the boards. The boards also swayed and sank down into the water when he stepped on them.

"You have to keep a sharp look out in here. We frequently see cotton mouth water moccasins. Sometimes they sleep on the boards. Just don't step on one if you can help it." Tommy said with an impish grin.

Greg was intimidated at first by this latest information, but soon realized that the other boys, who were now his new friends, were not really concerned themselves, and they came down here often to fish. After about twenty minutes of walking, jumping and balancing on the springy boards, and sometimes having to walk in the shallow water, they emerged, out from under the shadowed darkness. created by the canopy of trees. They stepped out in to a bright, open space of sunshine, and there was the lake. In the vast expanse of bright light and clear, blue, cloudless sky was the lake he had heard so much about, and had been so eager to see. The lake was surrounded by tall, crowded cypress trees. It was the size of seven or eight football fields. It was lined all the way around by tall green grasses and reeds that were head high. Further back from the water's edge, the ever present cypress trees began. The trees stood tall and thick surrounding the lake. Greg knew how thick they were, he had just walked through one part of the forest of trees. Standing on the shore you could not see over the reeds. The path of boards led to a small dock built out over the water. It was a narrow, short dock. Six boys could maybe stand crowded on it to fish. In the water, on the right side of the dock, was a row boat with two oars in it. It was tied to a tree stump beside the path.

"Do we fish from the dock or do we go out in the boat?" Greg asked, as he walked out on the dock, testing it.

"We should take the boat. There is a second lake connected to this one, and I think the fishing is better there most of the time. We want to show it to you any way." Tommy said.

"The smaller lake is one of my favorite places on the ranch." said Matt.

They loaded their poles and themselves into the boat. They paddled the boat, canoe style, to the other side of the lake. As they approached the other side, Greg could see a break in the tall reeds where there was a narrow water way passage going off to the right. He found that they could, by sometimes paddling and sometimes pulling their way, using the reeds, reach the other lake. The narrow water way was about thirty feet long. The second lake was two thirds the size of the larger one. The cypress trees seemed taller here. The reeds more green. They formed a perfectly circular wall around the lake. There was no wind and the surface of the water was still and perfectly flat. Across the lake, they could see an occasional turtle's head pop up and peer around. The water of the lake was dark black with a slightly reddish hue. It was so dark that it did not allow perception of any under water objects.

"What's this bottom like?" Greg asked.

"It's the same in all these swamp lakes, mostly mud and silt. I don't think you could stand up on the bottom. It's too mushy and you would sink right down. It's too creepy for me. I don't like how it feels when my feet touch down. I don't like to swim here either, because of that." Tommy said.

"Yeah but there are plenty of fish here, so let's see what we can catch today." Matt said.

They baited their hooks by piercing the plump wiggling worms along their length, several times. They each dropped the baited hooks over the side and sat back to watch their corks. Greg used this quiet time to take in the beauty and serenity of the lake and the fortress of tall trees. There were two buzzards circling in soaring spirals high above them. There was a very large bird sitting motionless, in the tallest of the cypress trees, across the lake. Greg thought he could see some tufts of feathers on each side of the head. It might be a great horned owl, he thought to himself. He knew that most fishermen did not like to talk while they were fishing, so he used the opportunity to study his new friends.

Tommy was bigger than Greg. He weighed twenty pounds more. He seemed to be very much at ease with himself here at the ranch. He had dark brown hair, almost black. His eyes were also deep brown. He had thick dark eyebrows, and long eyelashes. He had a good sense of humor and liked to joke around a lot. He had a space between his two front teeth and sometimes he had a slight, wispy, whistling sound to his voice as he spoke, and the air passed between his teeth. His nose curved significantly to the right side. Greg felt that he liked Tommy quite a bit already.

He turned his attention to Matt, who was intently watching his cork, almost hypnotically fixated. Matt was Greg's size. He was the same age as Greg. He had blond hair, it was wavy and thick. His eyes were a light blue color. He had a long, straight, delicate nose. He was what some people would definitely call a "pretty boy", Greg thought. He liked to talk a lot, and he liked to have fun, and when he said anything, he had a way of sniffing quickly through his nose, as if to emphasize the significance of his statement. He was fun to be with, because he liked to laugh, and he liked to joke and kid around.

As Greg looked around he thought to himself how beautiful this smaller lake was, and what a perfect spot it was for fishing from the boat. Greg immediately sensed within himself, what a wonderful feeling it was just being here. It was a special place to him already. He looked into the water, trying to see beneath the impenetrable surface. It was impossible, and he wondered briefly if there was not something more to the ranch story, something beneath the surface, something impenetrable to comprehend and understand.

"Is it possible there is something more to all of this? Is there something not so obvious, something wrong What could possibly be wrong with this wonderful place, is it all too good to be true? But so far, it is all true, and it is beautiful, and I am here." he thought to himself.

Just then, he heard a duck quacking. When he looked in the direction of the quacking duck, he saw it lifting off from the water. It was near the reeds, on the other side of the lake. The wings were beating rapidly as it climbed up off the water. As it climbed higher, it circled and then turned suddenly in their direction. As the duck passed over them, they could clearly hear the loud, blunt flapping sound of the rapidly beating wings. It cleared the tops of the trees near them, and then it was out of sight. Almost simultaneously,

Greg could see in his peripheral vision the owl launch it self out of the tree, and head in their direction, clearly in pursuit. The duck was now out of site, hidden by the tall trees. It was still quacking repeatedly. The owl now flew over their heads, but to their surprise, they could hear no flutter from its wings. It was as silent as the quietness in the boat. The owl now also disappeared behind the trees, in the same direction as the duck. The quacking continued for another five-seconds. Then there were several louder, quicker quacks, all of which sounded more desperate in tone, and then it was quiet again over the lake. In another ten-seconds the owl came back into view. It flew directly over them. The boys could see the duck in the talons of the owl, it was not moving. The boys could clearly see the orange bill, the green head, white neck band, and rusty colored breast. As it flew over them, again there was no sound from the owl's beating wings. The owl flew back to the same tree it had occupied; back to the same perch. After a few moments of looking around, It began with what seemed like controlled urgency, to tear into the duck with its beak. As it ate on the duck, it looked up and around from it's perch, between bites. The boys now all looked at each other in disbelief.

"I've never seen any thing like that." said Tommy.

"Me either." said Matt.

Greg was silent, still staring at the owl, eating the duck. After a few seconds he said,

"That was definitely a Mallard duck, from its markings. Don't you think guys?"

"I can say it was definitely a duck," said Tommy with a wink.

"That was really something. I've never seen anything like It." said Matt.

On this beautiful day, and with what just happened, this was no longer just another Florida lake to Greg, it was one of the most beautiful places he could remember seeing. He felt like he was made to be here, that somehow, this was all meant to be, and he was meant to be here too.

He liked his new friends. This type of life was nothing like his life back in the city. There he was alone the majority of the time, as his parent's worked long hours. There were no other boys in his neighborhood. He had no means of transportation, other than the city bus, so he had to entertain himself with library books and his imagination. He was not into the girl thing yet; not that he did not think about them. He often thought about what it would be like to hold one's hand, or to kiss a girl, but he knew it was a little early in his life yet. He knew he would be ready when the time came. He was already beginning to steal glances at some of the girls, and noting to himself if he thought they were attractive, or if they had any other interesting features such as large breasts or an interesting personality. For now he was happy to have these new friends, and to be here at the ranch.

In the next fifteen minutes they each had several bites, and Greg said, "Oh boy! This is going to be fun." Over the next couple of hours the three of them caught a dozen good sized catfish. When the first one was brought in to the boat, Tommy showed Greg how they broke the dorsal spines off with a pair of pliers, so as not to be impaled, since they were all barefoot. He said that you have to be really careful of the spines because if it went into your hand or foot, it was very painful and could cause a bad infection. Before they stopped fishing they had caught seven war-mouth perch and five bream all of them big enough to make a meal for one person, and they still had worms left over. Back at the dock they removed the guts from each fish by making an incision from the urogenital opening up to the gills. They scooped the intestines out with their fingers and threw them into the water at the edge of the reeds.

"These guts will make the fish and turtles get bigger for the next time we come fishing." said Tommy.

"Yeah, and it draws the snakes over here too." said Matt, looking at Tommy and then at Greg, with a concerned look on his face.

"Sometime you have to take the bad with the good." Tommy said with a big grin, and then added. "We didn't get a turtle this time but when we catch a big one, it can make a full meal. They are much harder to clean though."

When they finished cleaning the fish, Greg stood on the dock and looked out over the lake. Half way across the lake, he saw something swimming away from them.

"Hey guys, look at this. What is that?" Greg asked.

"I don't know what it is. I can't tell from here. Let's go take a closer look." said Tommy.

They piled into the boat in a hurry, and started paddling fast across the lake. When they were half way there Tommy stood up in the bow, trying to see what it was.

"That's a rabbit swimming across the lake. I didn't think rabbits could swim." said Tommy.

"That rabbit can swim. Look at him go." said Matt.

"Let's get him." said Tommy.

They gave chase, changing paddlers when required by tiredness. When they were two boat lengths away, and preparing to hit it with a paddle, the rabbit made it to the closest clump of bushes. It climbed up and into them. It disappeared from their sight, as quickly as it had appeared.

"That was exciting giving chase like that." said Greg.

"It was fun getting so close to it. I'm glad it got away though. We really did not need to kill it. We have plenty of fish for tonight." said Tommy.

They rowed back across the lake. They had left their fish in the water near the shore. They left in a hurry to see what was swimming across the lake. As they approached the dock and their fish, they could see one of their perch being pulled up onto the shore by a large black snake. They sat in the boat and watched the snake take their fish and slither away into the thick bushes.

"That is a cotton mouth snake, and they are poisonous, so you want to stay away from one of those.", Tommy said.

When it was gone, they collected their remaining fish.

They used branches, cut from a near by tree. They chose small branches with a "Y" at the bottom, and threaded the long stem through the fishes' gills. They used these branches as a means to transport the fish back to the house. Once back at the house they removed the scales from the flat fish with a scaler, washed them off, and put them in the refrigerator. They then found Joe. He said he wanted to show them his new way to remove the catfish skins. Joe was still in the shop working on his project. He said the shed was probably the best place to skin them. He got a knife and sharpened it. He got two pair of pliers, a six penny nail and a hammer.

"I just learned this from my uncle. We caught a bunch of salt water catfish in the gulf of Mexico last week end, so he used this technique to deal with so many of them. I'll skin the first fish, then you can skin the rest of them. First I make a cut all the way around the throat. Next we take this nail and drive it through the head, fixing the fish to this post. Then we take the pliers and grab the skin on opposite sides of the body. Once we get it started, we simply pull straight down toward the tail like this." Joe said. After a little effort, the skin pulled down, and off the catfish, like taking off a tight fitting glove. The boys were delighted at how easy it was, because before, they had to cut the skin off, inch by inch, with a sharp knife, it was tedious, and it seemed to take forever. They each took turns on the remaining catfish, and by the time the last one was done they were all mildly proficient at it.

"Where is Skipper and the Parkers?" asked Tommy after they had cleaned and put away the fish and the fishing gear.

"They went over to the eastern side of the property to check on the fence, and Lindsey wanted Skipper to see something else." Joe said.

"We need to talk with Mrs. Parker about fixing dinner, but I guess we'll have to wait until they get back. How do you like your fish cooked Joe?" Tommy asked.

"I like them the way Mrs. Parker does them. Plenty of flower, eggs and cornmeal and cooked in hot oil. Maybe we can sweet talk her into making some hushpuppies too. If you guys will behave nice." Joe said, smiling at them.

"Grits would be good too." Matt said.

The two boys then started showing Greg around the tool shed, and the old Ford truck, while Joe resumed work on his project.

CHAPTER 17

THE PASTURE

SUDDENLY, LINDSEY CAME RUSHING into the shed, he was clearly in a hurry, and he was out of breath.

"I'm glad you boys are all here. We've got us a big problem over in the east pasture. We need to get some chains and some big ropes. Joe, You crank up the truck and back it out. We'll get the chain and ropes. We need to get back out there as fast as possible, so let's all ride in the truck. One of you tie that dog up to the post. We don't want him out there with us now." he said.

With in a few minutes they were all in the truck, bouncing over the scattered patches of rough terrain, at Lindsey's urging they drove fast, dodging around the bigger clumps of palmetto bushes. The boys, riding in the bed of the pick up, were bounced around even as they clung to the wooden side rails. In ten minutes they could see Mrs. Parker, she was standing in a small clearing. She was looking down. Soon they could see Skipper. He was down on his knees. He was bending over a cow with a large belly. The cow was stretched out flat on her left side. She did not appear to be moving. As they drove up the cow lifted her head, and looked at them, but she did not try to get up. Then Skipper stood up, and indicated they should park the truck behind the cow, facing away.

"Any thing new happen since I left?" Lindsey asked as he dismounted from the truck.

"Not much, it maybe moved a couple of inches; that's about it." Skipper said.

"What's going on Skipper?" asked Joe as he walked over to Skipper.

"Step over here Joe, you other boys too, I'll show you our situation. We have been expecting her to throw her calf any day now. Lindsey has been checking on her daily. It looks like her time has come to give birth, but so far, the calf is not coming out on it's own. We may have to help her get it out, or we could lose both of them. Our quandary is when to intervene, and what to do when we do. She has been down all afternoon, and is losing her strength rapidly. I don't think she can stand up on her own right now. You can see the calf's feet sticking out a bit if you come over here. Greg and the other boys crept up behind the cow. Joe grabbed the cows tail and pulled it up over her back, toward her head. Greg could see the anus where some material was oozing out; a little more with each of the cows exertions. He could also see what he assumed was the cow's vagina. It looked like there were two sticks protruding from it. Greg had never seen a cow's vagina, and he was amazed at how big it was. He was also intrigued by the glistening pinkness. As the evening progressed, he became impressed by it's plasticity as well. It definitely got dilated and stretched out by the calf. From the center of the vagina he could see, as he looked closer, what looked like a calf's two hooves. They were sticking out about nine inches from the pink, glistening opening. At times the legs would protrude a little further out, and then retract back in again. This apparently happened in cadence with the labor movements.

"What are we going to do?" Joe asked as he stood up and looked around at the others.

"I'm not sure yet, but we may have to try to pull it out with the truck. That's what the chain and ropes are for, if nothing else works." said Skipper.

"I heard that in humans some times they have to cut into the belly with a knife and take the baby out." Tommy said.

"Yes, that's true Tommy, but we can't do that here. We don't have the anesthesia, the surgical instruments or knowledge of the anatomy in a cow. The only reason for us to do that now, is if the cow is dead or dying and there is a chance to save the calf. This calf may already be dead, so my plan now is to try to save the life of the cow, and maybe get a live calf out of it too. So here is my first thought. Joe you are the biggest and strongest. You and I will grab the legs with our hands and pull together. We'll pull at the same time it's being pushed out by the cow." said Skipper.

"O.K. Skipper, you say when." said Joe.

They made several coordinated efforts and did succeed in getting the legs out, almost to the hips. But that was as far as it would come. Greg was in an excited state of awe, staring wide eyed at the entire proceedings. He had never been involved in any thing like this before, not even during his times in Georgia, where farm animals were around all the time. He was very alert and alive with excitement, and he hoped he would be called on to help in some way. It soon became apparent that no further progress could be accomplished this way. When the Skipper stood up he was breathing hard and was short of breath.

"O.K. lets get on to plan two. Lindsey, you drive the truck when we get it hooked up to the calf. You boys hook that chain on to the truck. Probably the rear axel is the best place, don't you think Lindsey?

"Yeah, that's best on this truck." Lindsey said.

"O.K. then, lets get that rope attached to the chain. Make it about ten feet from the truck to the cow." said Skipper. When they were all connected, Lindsey climbed in the truck. He put it in first gear and when Skipper gave the go ahead signal, the truck began inching forward until the chain and rope were stretched tight.

"Now give it some gas!" he shouted. The truck began to move forward as the engine revved up and Lindsey let out on the clutch. As Greg watched, he could see the legs begin to move out of the cows vagina. They came out very, very slowly, until finally the hips began to emerge, and then it stopped.

"Gun it more!" shouted Skipper.

The engine noise increased and the truck started moving forward again. The rope stretched tight, and the cow started moving, sliding over the ground following the truck.

"Stop!" yelled Skipper.

"What's wrong?" asked Lindsey, as he climbed from the truck.

"You're dragging the cow with you." said Joe.

"O.K. then we need to tie the cow to that biggest palmetto bush in front of her. Take that other rope, loop it under her front legs, and tie it around her upper body. Not too tight, just enough to keep her from moving." Skipper instructed.

While this was being done, Greg looked at Mrs. Parker. She was walking around in circles, stopping to look every now and then, and mumbling something under her breath. All considered, she seemed pretty cool about everything, Greg thought. When the rope was secured to the base of the palmetto bush, it was time to try again. Lindsey climbed back in the truck, put it in gear, and when Skipper gave the word, he raced the engine and let out on the clutch. The truck began moving forward again. The chain and rope tightened. As the engine noise increased and the truck moved forward, the cow moved with the truck until the forward rope stopped her. So far the calf had not come any farther out of the cow.

"Stop! Put the brakes on. Let me check the tension on the chain." He felt the chain and then checked where the rope was attached to the calf's legs.

"All right, lets try this again." he said. The engine noise increased, the lines went tighter everywhere. The rear wheels suddenly began spinning and throwing sand and gravel backwards.

"Give it all she's got!" he yelled loudly. The engine noise increased more, the wheels started spinning again, more dirt started flying and spraying backwards. The noise from the truck's engine racing, the spinning tires, and the flying dirt spraying everything behind the truck, including the cow, created a loud and frightful scene. Slowly the calf began to emerge. It was very slow at first, then it was half out, and then suddenly it slid completely out of the cow. This was accompanied by a loud sucking sound they could barely hear over the engine and tire noise. The calf was now being dragged, it bounced along on the ground behind the truck until Lindsey got the word it was all over, and stopped the truck. A quick inspection showed there was no life in the calf. They quickly loosened the forward rope and inspected the cow. She was breathing shallow, spasmodic breaths. The heart beat was rapid, but felt strong. Soon she started breathing more regularly. The afterbirth soon emerged, and they helped by pulling it the rest of the way from her body and out through the vagina, the bleeding soon stopped, and she lay there not moving. There did not seem to be any thing torn externally on inspection of the vagina.

"The question now is whether she has any thing torn or injured internally. We may not know the answer to that for a few hours or even a day from now." said Skipper.

Mrs. Parker said, "I'll bring some water and grain out for her, and we will hope for the best.

"The boys can do that for you." said Skipper. "In the mean time I don't see any reason not to take the calf in to the shed, and butcher it for the freezer. It's still warm and there is nothing wrong with it anatomically. No evidence of an infection that I can see. Lindsey used to be a butcher of some renown in the old days. So, Joe and Greg, do you think you can handle that chore with Lindsey? Just listen to his instructions, and do what he says. I'll be there some of the time with you." Both boys got big grins on their faces and said at the same time.

"You can count on us Skipper."

"Tommy and Matt can help Mrs. Parker bring the water and grain back out. We'll see if we can keep her alive through the night. Maybe we should put a blanket over her tonight; she's been through a stressful ordeal today."

When they all got back to the house it was after eight o'clock. Lindsey decided it would be better to simply clean and quarter the calf. They harvested the heart, liver, pancreas, and other organs. He wanted to refrigerate it over night, and butcher it in the morning, when they were not so tired. When she returned from the field Mrs. Parker said that so far the cow had not tried to get up. The boys all said they would check on her again before going to bed.

It was time to make something for dinner. They had harvested the internal organs of the calf, so they could choose between the fish they caught earlier, or they could have kidneys, calf liver, heart or pancreas.

Every one preferred fish for the meal. The events of the calf and cow adventure was a little too fresh in their minds. The cutting up of the calf, and the harvesting process made the thought of eating some of it unappetizing to the boys. They feasted on fried fish, grits, hushpuppies, creamed corn and day old corn bread. For desert they had honey or strawberry jam on the corn bread with a glass of milk. After dinner they sat around talking about the excitement of the day's adventure. They were satisfied among themselves, that there was nothing more they could have done, considering the circumstances." Who wants sweetbread for tomorrow?" asked Mrs. Parker.

"How do you make the bread sweet? With honey?", asked Greg.

"No, it is not the kind of bread you are used to. I have a special recipe for cooking the calf's pancreas. It is a delicacy in some parts of the world. Sweetbread is what it is called." she said.

"I'll eat anything, any body else will eat." said Greg.

"All right then, I will make my special dish for everyone tomorrow." said Mrs. Parker.

Skipper and Lindsey said they looked forward to her specialty dish, they both liked eating sweetbreads. They did not get to eat them very often. The boys were not quite so certain. It showed on their faces.

It was half past ten that night when all four boys went back, with flash lights, to check on the cow. She was still on her side when they got to her. She opened her eyes when they approached. She raised her head and made an effort to get up, but she could not get to her feet. They offered her water and she drank some of it, but did not try to eat. They covered her again, refilled the water tub and left her for the night. When they got back to the house, they found that the Parkers had gone to bed already. The boys were too tired and sleepy to take a bath. When they went in the bedroom, Skipper told Greg he could have the cot next to the window. Joe would sleep in the other cot, and Tommy and Matt would sleep in the big bed. Greg stripped down to his underwear, climbed under the covers, and began looking out of the window above his head, he could see the full moon, rising slowly, coming into his view. He watched the moon for a long while, thinking about how wonderful his life had suddenly become. He thought about the day, and how exciting it had been; fishing in the magical lake, seeing the owl catch and eat the duck, getting the calf out, and butchering it. He told himself that he much preferred being here at the ranch than at his home, where he was by himself most of the time, with nothing to do but read. He liked reading books from the library, but this was a much more exciting life. Here he was living life in stead of reading about it. He thought briefly of Matt and Tommy sleeping in the bed with Skipper. He wondered if it meant any thing, or had any hidden significance. The next thing he knew, he was hearing his name being called, followed by, "You better get a move on or your gonna miss breakfast."

CHAPTER 18

NEXT DAY

After breakfast they all got in the truck and drove to where the cow was last night. She was not there, and was no where to be seen.

"She must have gotten up and wandered away. It looks like she ate some of the grain we left." said Skipper. They drove around for a short while looking for her, but never found her.

"We'll come back later this afternoon." said Skipper. "I planned on taking the boys fishing today. I wanted to go over to the old pier at New Port Ritchie to do some salt water fishing." Skipper said. "Now we need to butcher that calf. So we will have to put that off until next week end. If we all work on that butchering project together, we can finish it by early afternoon."

Back at the house they got the calf quarters out and all of them learned how to cut the different parts of the calf in to steaks, roasts and chops. They wrapped the different steaks in packages of twos and fours. They wrapped the roasts according to sizes. They wrapped some of the ribs separately. They planned on having some of them for dinner. Through out the project they all had a good time together. They were laughing and joking with each other about how they were now apprentice butchers, and that there must be a merit badge for butchering. The pieces that were not good enough to be wrapped separately, they put into a separate container. Lindsey said he knew a man down the road a bit who could make sausages out of all the pieces. The bones were set aside for soups. The better pieces of leftover red meat they planned to make hamburgers from, so they got out the meat grinder and made two packages of six burgers each. For lunch they had fresh calf liver and onions, boiled potatoes and a salad. Mrs. Parker prepared her sweetbread dish. Of the boys, only Joe really liked them. All the adults enjoyed them, very much. They planned barbecued ribs for dinner, with French fries and coleslaw. When they cleaned up from butchering the calf, it was late afternoon. The boys decided to go exploring around the ranch. They would try to find the cow while they were out. They would definitely be back in time for the barbecued ribs dinner because they had to get the fire ready for cooking them, and to prepare the French fries for Mrs. Parker to cook. They also had to chop up the cabbage for the Cole slaw. That was how things were done at the ranch. Every one pitched in and contributed their fair share of the work. Here at the ranch they were happy to do so. Those were the rules Skipper set up from the very beginning. No one ever complained, and no one ever felt put upon by these simple rules.

The boys explored a large part of the dry part of the ranch that afternoon. There were three different cypress tree swamps scattered on the property. There was a small open lake, the size of a football field, with no trees on the high side of the property. It was a very shallow lake, and there were times when it almost dried up at certain times of the year. No one ever thought about fishing in it. There were several wading birds feeding along the shore that took flight as they approached. The day was warm. The sky was filled with mixed cloud formations. There were some large fluffy clouds that looked like puffs of cotton candy. As they walked around the lake and approached a clump of thick palmetto bushes, the cow suddenly stood up and looked at them, calmly chewing on her cud. The boys were happy to see her. They congratulated each other on finding her alive. On the way back to the house they discussed the whole event. They were all still excited about what they had seen. The noise of the truck and the dirt flying everywhere was quite a spectacle. They discussed their minor role in saving the cows life. Eventually they got around to talking about how it was really

Skipper that deserved all the credit, and it made them proud he was their scout master. They also talked about how happy they all were that they could be at the ranch. Here, they could learn about doing different things, and actually do some things they would never have an opportunity to do back in the city.

Back at the house they happily told every one about seeing the cow, and about how excited they were to find her alive. Mrs. Parker was particularly happy, for now she would have fresh milk at the ranch for a while. She would have to start milking her soon. The boys started the fire in the pit they used for outdoor cooking. They wanted the fire to burn down enough to get coals to cook the ribs. Inside they chopped the cabbage and onions for the coleslaw. They then sliced the potatoes for the French fries. When they had every thing prepared Mrs. Parker said,

"I don't know how I can get along next week without all this help preparing dinner. You boys must be a big help to your mothers when you are at home?" No one said anything right away. They all looked at one another, waiting to see who would speak up first. Finally Tommy said,

"I try to be as helpful as I can, but, to be honest, I don't help as much at home as I do here."

"Me either." said Greg. "but I think I will be much more helpful around the house from now on. I'm happy you brought the subject up." he added. He was already thinking about what different kinds of things he could do around his house. He realized now, he wanted to keep his mother happy with him in the future, so that she would not prevent him from coming back to the ranch.

Lindsey cooked the ribs perfectly. The dinner was a huge success. Everyone ate as much as they could hold. While they were having their milk and cornbread for desert, Skipper said,

"We have to get up early tomorrow morning. When we stay at the ranch on Sunday nights, we get to bed early, because we get up early. I want to make sure I get each one of you home in time to be ready for school. We don't want any thing to interfere with being on time. Get your things together tonight. We'll have a breakfast of toast and cereal, and be out of the door and on the road by six. We want every thing to go smoothly, because we want to keep the parents happy. You need to get to school on time, have plenty of sleep, be alert and learn as much as possible to keep those grades up. By keeping your parents happy, it helps them to understand how beneficial it is for you to come to the ranch"

CHAPTER 19

A NEED TO CONVINCE

When Greg got home Monday morning he was excited to tell his mother and stepfather about his week end. He quickly told them about the Parkers, the ranch, the fishing, the owl catching the duck, the cow event, and about how much he was looking forward to returning to the ranch the next weekend. They were going to go salt water fishing at New Port Richie.

"Not so fast young man. We will have to see about that. We need to do a lot more talking about this going off on the weekends before we can make that kind of decision. Right now, you get ready for school." said his mother.

On the bus, on his way to school, Greg thought about what his mother had said. He realized now, if he wanted to be able to go to the ranch on the weekends, he would need to somehow convince his mother it was a good for everyone when he was allowed to go to the ranch. He would somehow have to convince his mother how beneficial it was for him specifically. It was true that it was his best opportunity to learn about camping, scouting and outdoor skills. There was always an adult around at the ranch, so his behavior would be monitored. She would have to understand that the boys were always on their best behavior or they would not be invited back. It was a good place to start accumulating his merit badges, so he could become a life Scout and maybe even an Eagle Scout. He decided he was going to make sure that she realized he was a much better son when he was at home from now on. He would do the dishes without having to be reminded. He would take out the garbage and do the lawn work on his own. He would keep his room and the rest of the house clean and picked up. He would show her how he had become a better boy, by being more helpful, more concerned about the house. He would make these changes for the better, because he hoped it would convince his mother, and improve his chances of being allowed to spend his weekends at the ranch. That was where he wanted to be. He would make sure his mother realized how beneficial it was for her and her husband when he was allowed to be at the ranch. He was successful, because she allowed him to go the next weekend.

As the weeks and months went by, he was allowed to spend most of his weekends at the ranch. His change in behavior and his attitude when at home was very obvious. His school grades improved. He becamea model of the perfect boy. He never created problems of any kind for his mother. He was never argumentative or confrontational. He was polite and courteous. Because of these noticeable improvements in his behavior and his improved school grades, his mother became more and more lenient about the ranch. His weekends and holidays became a whirlwind of activities, filled with fishing, swimming, boating, exploring, learning and having fun.

On the drives to the ranch, or when driving to go fishing in the waters around the piers and the bridges of the New Port Ritchie area, the boys practiced and learned the Morse Code by studying together. They challenged each other over and over about the various dits and dahs of the alphabet. They studied together for the various merit badges they were pursuing. Some nights they went shrimping in the grassy shallow waters of the salt water bays. They used flash lights to shine up the bright pink eyes of the shrimp, hiding in the grasses, and then scoop them up with wire rimmed nets on the end of long poles.

Some nights they went lake fishing with the Parkers. There was another of their favorite lakes near by they could drive to. It had a gentle sloping shoreline on which they could camp and beach the boat. They set out a trot line across the lake. The line would have a dozen or more snoods with hooks, that were spaced three feet apart along the length of it. Each one of the snood's hooks would be baited with worms or different chicken and fish parts. They would row out to check the trot line several times during the night. They frequently needed to take the caught fish off, and rebait the empty hooks. These were incredibly fun nights for the boys. Mrs. Parker made hot coffee over an open fire. She put the coffee grounds into the boiling water, and when it was ready she poured the coffee through a strainer in to their cups. The coffee was always delicious. It was strong and flavorful, and when they added the cream and honey, it was the best coffee they ever remembered having. It was always exciting to row out to the trot line in the darkness of night. They carried flash lights with them, and when they shined their beams out over the lake, they would always see many pairs of eyes, that looked like twin burning cigars, sitting side by side, shining back at them from out in the distance. They were startled at first to learn they belonged to alligators. Their apprehension subsided with time, because the alligators never caused them any kinds of problems.

They never knew what kind of fish they would find on the hooks. The pulling and jerking motion of the trot line became more vigorous as the boat approached. Usually it was an eclectic mixture of many different types of fish. They caught large and small mouth Bass, catfish, gar, trout and occasionally they would catch turtles. Sometimes there were hard shelled turtles, and sometimes soft shelled turtles. It was always an activity filled with fun, excitement and definitely surprises. The boys all grew much closer to the Parkers through their shared adventures. They became a type of extended family unit, working together to take care of the ranch, the house, the animals, and they also shared in the fun of their now exciting lives. Life at the ranch was, for the boys, an opportunity to live beyond the limitations imposed by life in the city.

CHAPTER 20

SUMMER PLANS

TOWARD THE END OF the school year, Skipper began to talk about upcoming summer plans. He was particularly interested in knowing which of the boys would like to be at the ranch for the summer. His plans included finding a house on the salt water, some where along the gulf coast, not too far from the ranch. Who ever was staying at the ranch, would also be involved in building a boat that would eventually stay at the new house on the water. It would be built at the ranch, where they had all of the tools and equipment they would need. He wanted the boat to be large enough to take several of the Boy Scout Troop members out in the Gulf of Mexico, for fishing expeditions. He wanted it to be available to the troop members in the years to come. It promised to be an interesting and very busy summer. The boys would be living with the Parker's at the ranch house. There was going to be plenty of hard work for everyone living at the ranch. Skipper would only be at the ranch on the week ends, as he worked at the base during the week days. He was still a major in the air force, and had several years before he could consider retirement. He made it very clear that the boys would be answerable to the Parkers when he was not there. He also made it clear that any one who made it difficult for the Parkers, or caused them problems of any kind, would not be welcome at the ranch anymore. Greg knew immediately that he wanted to be one of the boys who stayed at the ranch that summer. It thrilled him to think about being involved with building a big boat like Skipper was talking about. It did not take long for him to realize how disappointed he was going to be if his mother did not allow him to spend his summer at the ranch. He began planning the best way to present this request to her. He knew that his mother would never consider it if she did not talk to Skipper and all the persons involved. She would also want to get to know the Parkers as well. When he brought this new problem up with Skipper and the Parkers they said there was a solution, one they had used in the past.

"After you tell your parents that you would like to spend some of the summer with us here at the ranch, all of us will make an appointment to meet with them. We will take the other boys along so they can meet every one who will be here, and involved with the summer projects. This is what we have done in the past, and it usually takes away most concerns parents may have. It is usually successful, unless they already have some specific and different plans for you." said Skipper.

When Greg first told his mother and stepfather about the opportunity to spend the summer at the ranch, she was not at all happy about the idea. He continued talking about how great an opportunity this was going to be for him. He would be involved in building a boat with the other boys. This was something he really wanted to do he said. He talked about how much more fun and educational it would be for him instead of having to spend the summer by himself. He would be alone at the house during the days. He would be searching and trying to find different ways of entertaining himself. He talked honestly and convincingly of how much better it would be for him if he were at the ranch.

"Don't get your hopes up. I will meet and talk with Skipper and the others; we will make up our minds after we have those discussions.

Greg knew then that every thing would depend on how convincing Skipper, the Parkers and the other boys would be when they all met together to discuss the summer plans.

THE MEETING

When the big meeting was scheduled, the Parkers, Skipper, Joe, Tommy, and Matt came into the living room. Greg felt like the battle was possibly won from the beginning. The boys were all neat and clean. Their manners were impeccable, and they were convincing about how well they all got along together. They all talked of how excited they were to be able to have this opportunity to spend time working and learning together. The Parkers told his mother that they had known the Skipper for many years. They said that their own son, who was now in the Army in Officers Candidate School, had been rescued and set on the right path by the Skipper. He had been in trouble with the law on multiple occasions until he met Skipper. His association with Skipper had turned his life around. As a result of this, they had known and worked for the Skipper ever since. They were happy to have the boys at the ranch. They enjoyed having them around. They said they were comforted personally by knowing the boys would be safe and out of the way of potentially bad influences. They had personal experience with a situation that can tempt boys with too much time on their hands. The Skipper was his usual reassuring and commanding self. He was handsome and neat in his air force uniform. He was convincing that the boys were not only welcome, but, he was counting on them to do much of the work on the ranch, and on the boat they were all going to build together. It only took a few days for his mother to make up her mind. She finally consented and told him she would let him try it. She also made it clear, she would rescind her permission if there were ever problems of any kind. After this was decided, Greg thought that his mother must know how much better this would be for him and her. He thought it must be better for her and her relationship with her husband. He did not cause problems for them now, but they would have more time for themselves, and have more privacy for their own relationship. Greg was also beginning to think of the silliest thing. It would be great if his mother and Skipper were married to each other. Then he could have the best of both worlds, and maybe his mother would not have to work so much any more.

CHAPTER 21

SUMMER BEGINS

For Greg the summer at the ranch began a few days after school was over. Skipper drove the boys to the ranch on the first week end after school was out. Besides Greg, it was Joe, Tommy and Matt who received permission from their parents to live at the ranch with the Parkers for the summer. It was understood that Skipper would only be there on the week ends.

The first week end, all five of them drove west. They were heading over to Hudson. It was a forty-five minute drive from the ranch. Skipper told them he had been doing research on available houses on the water. He said that one located in Hudson appealed to him the most. When they arrived in Hudson, they turned left off of U.S. 19, on to the main street of town, and drove straight on through the residential area. The road stopped at the end of the paved street. Where the road ended, there was a two story house on the right hand side. On the other side of the house was the salt water. The house they were looking at was right on the water. They learned that the stretch of water in front of the house was the end of a long twisting arm of a bayou connecting to the Gulf of Mexico. They also learned that when they had the boat at the house, they could go right out into the Gulf to fish. They would be able to go every day, anytime they desired, weather permitting. There was a small, FOR SALE, sign in the front yard. The house was a two story structure. It looked like it was built on stilts; there were no living accommodations on the first level. It must have been planned to be a garage, maybe a place for a car to be parked under the house, but there was no drive way leading under the house. There was a sea wall immediately in back of the house. Standing on the sea wall they looked out over the water way of the bayou, in back of the house. The salt water ended, and fresh water began about seventy feet to the right of the house. The sea wall they were standing on formed a "U" shape structure around the end of the bayou. In the center of the "U" shaped wall area, where the water ended, the surface of the water was roiling and swirling. It reminded Greg of the spring at the Sulfur Springs swimming pool he liked so much. There were thousands of gallons of fresh water, flowing up from the huge underground spring. Where the spring water flowed upout of the ground, the sea wall was about twenty-five yards wide. The sea wall and the water widened progressively more the further away from the spring, as it flowed toward the open water. Directly in front of the house, the sea wall on the other side was fifty yards away, and the width enlarged and widened rapidly the further away from the spring. The sea wall stopped just to the left of the front of the house, on their side of the bayou. The shore line beyond the sea wall was made up of tall grasses, bushes and reeds that extended to the first turn of the bayou towards the Gulf. At the widest the water in front of the house was a hundred yards across. As the group walked around the house, Skipper pointed out the empty area to the left of the house and wall. It would be a perfect place to construct the boat ramp. When the ramp and the boat were completed they could keep the boat on the ramp, out of the water. On the right side, looking out from the house, was a huge oak tree near the end of the sea wall. Some of the larger branches of the tree extended out over the spring. A thought immediately flashed in Greg's mind. This would be a fun place from which to drop into the water, or to tie a rope and make a swing. First they would have to determine how deep the water was where the spring came up out of the ground. Every one was already becoming excited about the possibilities for the unlimited amount of fun this beautiful piece of property could provide them. It was a great place. The location would allow them to swim, to keep a boat, and to fish, all of this ten feet in front of the house.

"Can we see the inside of the house?" Joe asked.

"Yes, they said a key could be found over here." said Skipper.

He walked over to the wooden stairs that led up to the entrance of the house. He reached under one of the steps and pulled out a key. After climbing the stairs, he opened the door, and they all walked single file in to the one room. It was a single large room, with an enclosed bathroom in the corner, opposite the entrance way. The kitchen area was on the same side as the stairway entrance. Toward the front there was a queen sized bed against the wall. Between the kitchen sink and the bed was a dining table that could seat six people. There was a door in the middle of the wall facing the water. There was a window on each side of the door. When they walked out of the door, there was an eight foot deep balcony, the length of the room. It looked out over the entire arm of the bayou, and the spring. From the balcony, they could hear the rushing, swirling sounds of the water from the surface of the spring.

"We could put some double decker bunks against the wall over there." said Skipper, indicating the wall opposite the dining table.

"We would have four to six more bunks where people could sleep."

"Wow Skipper! Do you really think it's possible we could get something like this? It would be perfect for what you've been talking about." asked Greg. "It's definitely a possibility, and I will check on it immediately, as soon as I get back to town. I agree with you boys; It will be perfect for what we need, and want to do." said Skipper.

CHAPTER 22

HUDSON HOUSE AND THE BOAT

When Skipper returned to the ranch the following Friday night he called a group conference. Every one including the Parkers gathered around the dinner table. Skipper got a very serious look on his face and said,

"I have some news that affects every one here." He was silent for a moment and then a large grin began to form on his face, and he said,

"We got it!".

"We got what?" asked Joe.

"We got that house on the water in Hudson that we looked at last week." said Skipper.

It took only seconds for this news to sink in to the crowd. Greg was the first one to cry out with a loud, "Whoopee" and he jumped up from the table and hugged Matt, who was closest to him. All the others stood up and started hugging each other, all the while smiling and congratulating each other, and the Skipper. When the excitement began to subside, Skipper said,

"O.k. every one, now listen up, here is my plan."

Skipper presented his ideas; Both his short and his long range plans. The general picture of his plan slowly emerged and took form in the minds of the boys and the Parkers. Now that the boat house acquisition had been accomplished, the building of the boat could begin. Skipper said he planned to take a two week vacation very soon. During that time they could acquire the materials for the construction of the boat. He said there was some spare plywood at the base where he worked, and it would be available to them. All they had to do was to pick it up. They would rent a large truck and move the materials out to the ranch. Skipper said that his brother, who was a building contractor, had agreed to be available at certain key times during the construction of the boat. He would be particularly helpful. His knowledge and special skills would be required for certain parts of the boat construction project. He would also arrange for them to have the necessary tools for the project. Skipper had already ordered a set of plans for the boat he wanted to build. They would build the boat in the back yard of the ranch, next to the tool shed. They could store the tools away at night, and in inclement weather. First they would build a frame, on which to construct the boat. It would be built on the trailer they would use to transport it to the water.

They could also now begin work on the construction of the boat ramp at the Hudson house. The boys would cut down and transport the necessary pine trees from the ranch property. Joe would drive the pick up truck after it was loaded with the cut up pine trees, to the boat house in Hudson. The pine trees sections and the train rails could be stored in the front yard during the construction of the boat ramp. The area of the yard for the boat ramp was immediately adjacent to the house. It could be prepared by excavation and grading. The boys could do this with shovels, hoes, pick axes and wheelbarrows. While the ramp construction was going on, the boys could all live at the boat house. He wanted the boys to also have some fun time during the summer, so Skipper would acquire a row boat for them to use to go fishing and exploring when they were not working. The row boat could be moored off the sea wall, in front of the house, or even pulled up on to the graded ramp when that portion of the project was completed. As Skipper unveiled his ideas and plans for the summer projects, Greg was beginning to formulate and visualize in his mind what a spectacular summer this was going to be. It was exciting to imagine what his life was going to be like; living at the ranch, with all of its beautiful open wilderness and swamp lands to explore. In addition to the lakes at the ranch, there were other larger lakes within a few miles of the ranch in which to fish and swim.

When they were not at the ranch, they would be staying at the boat house where they would have unlimited access to swimming and fishing from right in front of the house. They were also going to have a boat of their own from which to fish and explore. He knew he would have to work hard physically sometimes, at both places, he knew that, but even the work time would be fun and enjoyable he thought. He would be working side by side with some of his best and closest friends, they would all be working and sharing in the effort together. How could his life get any better than this? He thought to himself.

CHAPTER 23

WORK BEGINS

THE NEXT DAY SKIPPER and the boys toured the stand of pine trees, they planned to use, together. They selected and marked the trees that would be cut down to be transported to the boat house. Joe would be in charge of this phase of the plans. He would be driving the truck, and he would be the final word on the number of logs, and the size of the load for each trip. He was certainly the oldest, but he was also, by temperament, the most steady and reliable. He was always the serious one in the group, and Skipper made it clear from the beginning that he was in charge when they were away from the Parkers. Whatever Joe said was to be observed, acknowledged and followed by the other boys. Discussions among them were allowed and acceptable, but Joe would always have the final word.

Skipper would be back in two weekends with the truck and the first load of lumber. When that load was delivered and unloaded, they all would drive back to Mac Dill Air Force base and collect more wood and the plywood for the boat's construction. In three weekends Skipper would begin his vacation. They would all start together on the construction of the boat when he was there full time. While he was gone this next two weeks, the boys could cut down the trees, section them into lengths, and haul them over to the boat house in Hudson. If there was any time left after hauling the trees, they could start on grading the boat ramp bed. This was another project they could do without skilled supervision.

They went to work on Monday morning. They were able to fell the chosen trees on the first two days. The next day they cut them into six foot lengths. Lindsey stayed with the boys during this phase. He offered constructive comments but, he let the boys and Joe do all the work. Loading the logs into the truck bed was the most challenging part. With Lindsey's suggestions they used two four to one pulleys to help load the logs into the truck. They attached the pulleys to the stoutest branch of a big tree. By parking the truck under the tree, they could suspend the logs enough to maneuver them into the truck bed. Joe and Lindsey kept checking the springs under the truck, and finally decided that five logs was the most they could carry at a time. At the boat house, they secured the logs to a stout post and drove out from under them. They then rolled them into a separate pile for storage. Over the next seven days they moved all the logs over to Hudson.

After the last load was delivered, Joe made the decision to take a couple of days off from work. He said he wanted them all to have some time to swim and fish in the waters in front of the house. This was when Greg found out that the depth of the water, where the spring came up out of the ground under the tree, was thirty to thirty-five feet deep. There was no way any of them could get to the bottom. Even if they could dive that deep, the current of the spring was too powerful for them to swim very deep against it. In front of the house, the depth became much more shallow, only fifteen to twenty feet deep. Slightly further out, the underwater scene changed abruptly. Just past the house, in the direction of the outlet to the Gulf, the depth became seventy to eighty feet or more. Even with the clear water and goggles on, they were barely able to the other side of the shoreline. It was like a huge underwater room with steep walls. There was a large number of what appeared to be caves in the steep walls of the huge pool. There were multiple ridges of wall like structures, five to fifteen feet high, coming up from the bottom, and off of the sides. This was a fish paradise Greg thought. They could see large number of snapper, grouper and the striped sheeps heads swimming in and out of the cave like structures. The most spectacular thing they saw were large Gar like fish swimming around half way to the bottom. The Gar fish were almost as big as the boys. The boys all admitted later, that they felt a twinge of fear, and intimidation, being in the same waters with such large fish. They had no idea whether these kinds of fish ever attacked humans. So they decided that until they knew better, they would play it safe, and swim in front of the house, and over the waters of the spring, and not over the deeper water where the large fish were.

CHAPTER 24

JOE'S STORY

THAT NIGHT THEY SPENT their first night alone at the boat house. Joe had informed the Parkers of his plans to return to the ranch the following morning. They knew they needed to be back before noon, because Skipper was going to arrive early in the afternoon, with the truck and the first load of lumber. They would need to be there to help unload the truck. The following morning they were all going in the truck to the air force base to get more plywood, and they would all be needed to help load the plywood on to the truck. Joe had already made plans for their dinner. He brought it from the ranch, two packs of hot dogs, three cans of baked beans, some bacon and onions. He also brought a large pot. When night time came all of the four boys were really hungry from their day of swimming and exploring.

They put the cut up bacon and onions in the pot and cooked them until the aroma filled the room. Then they added all the beans and hot dogs in to the same pot, and cooked them together. When the beans and the franks started bubbling, they cooked them a little longer to make sure the franks were hot through and through. They opened the root beers they had purchased, for five cents each, on the drive over to Hudson. Each boy filled his own plate with as much hot dogs and beans as he could eat, grabbed a piece of buttered toast, and then they all sat down to enjoy one of their their favorite meals. It was a real treat to be on their own, cooking their own meals for themselves, and having the freedom to talk openly and honestly, without having to monitor their conversations for the adults. After dinner was over, they cleaned up their plates, silver ware and the pot, and sat down to a night of boys talk.

"That was a great dinner, Joe." Tommy said.

"My favorite meal." Greg said.

"Mine too." Matt added.

"What are you going to do next year, Joe? I know this will be your last year of junior high, so what high school will you attend?" Tommy asked.

"I don't know yet, my parents are talking about moving to Texas in another year. If they do move, I'll have to go with them." Joe said.

"Aw Joe, that's not good. What will we do without you? We'll have the boat finished by then. You won't be here to use it, if you have to leave." Tommy said.

"Yeah, but if they do move, I will have no choice." Joe said.

"Well, maybe they won't move." Matt said.

"What will be, is what will be." Joe said.

"How come your only in the ninth grade, and your sixteen years old, Joe?" Matt asked.

"Yeah, I know it's unusual. I caught the meningitis when I was six, and it took me a couple of years to recover from it. They weren't sure I was going to make it. They tell me I was in a coma for several weeks. It took a long time for me to get back to normal. After that school wasn't so easy for me, so I had to repeat a couple of grades."

"Wow! Joe, I would never have guessed you had to go through something like that." Greg said.

"Yeah, They say I'm back to normal now, but it was sure tough on me for a while. They thought maybe I would be retarded or something like that. The guys in school never gave me a hard time though, because I was so much bigger than any body else, and much stronger. It only took a couple of fights, and after that, I never had any more problems."

"Say Joe, what do you think about those really big fish we saw this afternoon?" Greg asked.

"They may be a type of Alligator Gar. Those are small ones. I've heard they can get up to three hundred pounds, and grow to ten feet long."

"Whoa Joe! I never want to see one that big, if I'm in the water." said Matt.

"Hey Joe, have you ever had anything to do with girls yet?" Greg asked.

"Like what?" Joe asked.

"You know, like have a girl friend, or kiss one, or do anything like that?" Greg asked. Tommy and Matt looked at Joe at the same time. They stared at him expectantly, while they waited to hear what his answer would be. The question had come so quickly, it was a complete surprise, and It definitely got all of their attention.

"Well, Yes, now that you ask. What do you guys really want to know?"

"Anything and everything. Any kind of stuff about sex, Joe?" Greg asked.

"What about the rest of you guys, you want to hear about that kind of stuff?" Joe asked.

They all quickly nodded their heads up and down, and said yes they did. Then they sat forward on the edge of their seats, anxiously waiting to hear what he would say next.

"Well, O.K., since it's just us boys here, I'll tell you about what happened to me one time. I was swimming with some of my older friends. You know that swimming pool in Sulfur Springs, we drive by it on the way to the ranch?" Every one nodded their heads.

"Yeah, I know it really good. I used to swim there a lot." Greg said.

"Well, then, after this story, you may never think of it the same way again. You know that water slide that goes from the big pool, and flows down the chute to the lower level? Right behind that water fall, just above the water, on the lower level, there 's a big flat ledge, and a type of cave. It's big enough for seven or eight guys. We boys had been swimming, and playing tag, most of the morning. Suddenly, my best buddy, swims up to me, real quick like, and grabs me by the arm. He says to me,

"Joe, we have to get up on that ledge behind the water fall. I mean, like right now. Come on get moving, follow me and don't say a word to anybody."

"So we swim over, we duck under the water fall, and climb up on the ledge behind the waterfall.

"Guess what we find?" Joe asked.

The boys all had a blank, and then an expectant look on their faces. "There is this girl standing there, along with two other guys I didn't know. She has long blonde hair and it's still wet from swimming. One of the guys steps over to her. The girl looks at this guy, and they start smiling at each other. She puts her arms around his neck and they start kissing. He moves his hands downwards. After that things started moving in a direction I have never seen before. I know I will never forget what I saw that day under the waterfall, and may never see anything like it again."

"Well Joe, what did you see?", Tommy asked.

"Nah guys, that is all I am going tell you. That is enough, you will just have to use your imaginations." Joe said.

"Wow Joe! I guess you have had something to do with girls." said Greg.

"Yeah, but remember guys, I'm a lot older than you. We better get some sleep now, we've got a big day coming up tomorrow.", Joe said.

CHAPTER 25

RESTING REFLECTIONS

THE BOYS GOT UP early so that they could have a swim in the cool, clear, fresh water of the spring, before heading back to the ranch. It was a beautiful morning. The blue skies were cloudless. The intense blue of the sky was also clear and clean, like the waters of the spring. The cool freshness of the morning was invigorating. The slight breeze coming out of the West, brought to their nostrils, the salt water smells of the Gulf, and the vegetation lining the shores along the stretch of bayou reaching out to the Gulf of Mexico. They talked excitedly with each other about how good it was going to be having a row boat in front of the house. This led them to talking about how much better it would be when they had the big boat they were building, tied up in front of the house.

After a long swim in the fresh cool waters rushing up from the deep spring, they made a pot of coffee. They made it like Mrs. Parker always did on their camping trips. They put the ground up coffee directly in the water, and brought it to a boil. They poured it through a strainer into their cups. The aroma was delightful, the flavor was strong and intense, with a taste of the earth. The color was a deep, rich, royal, dark brown. They used condensed canned milk for their cream, and honey from the ranch to sweeten it. While sitting on the balcony, and drinking the coffee they had made for themselves, they looked at each other, and out over the sunlit expanse of the waters of the bayou that stretched far out in front of the house. They talked about how lucky they were, and how wonderful it was to be here, at this house, and on the waters connecting them to the Gulf of Mexico. When they finished the big boat they could go out and fish in the Gulf of Mexico anytime they wanted.

Greg especially loved being at the house on the water. He loved every thing about it. The opportunity for fun and exploration of nature was unlimited, and it was beautiful there. He had always been a water person. When he was at the house he swam every day. He was a good swimmer, and was comfortable being in and around the water. He could dive deeper than most the other boys. He could hold his breath longer than the others, and he could swim further underwater. He found that Matt was not as comfortable in the water, and was much more cautious than the other boys. Greg eventually began to get the impression that Matt was envious of his swimming ability. This was a new experience for Greg. He had never been envied for anything. He had never been in a situation where there was a feeling of competition between himself and a friend. He did not dwell on this realization, but he was aware of its existence. It was also new for him, because he was never really better at any type of sports activities. When he participated in group sports, like base ball or basket ball, in school, or on the play grounds, he was never the first or second choice by the team leaders who were doing the choosing. He was also not ever the kind of player who got to be a team captain doing the choosing. That was the way it had been all of his life, that he could remember. He simply was not good at team sports; he knew and accepted that fact. So it was a new experience for him to be envied for his abilities.

"Just part of the growing up process." Greg thought.

The younger boys had now developed a new, deeper, and stronger sense of esteem for Joe. He was always their serious, somber leader, and the story he told the night before about his swimming pool experience, was still fresh in their minds. It captivated their imagination and heightened their esteem for Joe. They were all in the strong grip of their rising and surging hormone levels. The thoughts and images of the pretty girl Joe had described, and what happened was still fresh and intensely vivid in Greg's memories. Every time Greg thought about it, a huge sharp, ping of emotion surged through him, and quasi tumescent stirrings began. Each one of the boys had thought many times before, about what it would be like when they lost their own innocence; where, when, how and with whom, was always lurking in their minds. They knew it was a little soon for that type of life experience to happen to them, but every one of them had heard, maybe falsely, of boys their age having some type of unexpected experience occur. Theoretically, it could possibly happen at any time now, but Greg felt his turn must surely be a long way off, because he was still so ignorant about girls. He had no idea of what to talk to girls about, much less about how to dance with one. He had never even held a girl's hand. That other thing, that ultimate thing, that boys only whispered about would have to be blind, accidental luck, like what happened to Joe, at the swimming pool, behind the waterfall, for it to happen to him. He really envied boys like his cousin Jeryl in Georgia, and his new friend Bill. They seemed to be born with a magical knack for communicating and being friends with girls.

This thought made him think back on the time when he was in the fifth grade and going to school in Tampa. He had a crush on one of the plump neighborhood girls in his class room. He was walking the girl and her friends home from school one afternoon. One of the other boys who was walking with then started giving Greg a hard time, razzing him about his liking the girl. The argument escalated until Greg, in frustration, shot the other boy a pair of double birds, using the middle finger of both hands. The girl was so horrified and upset at Greg's crude, and disgusting ways, she forbade him to ever walk with her or talk to her again. He chuckled now at how embarrassed he was at the time. He had hurt her feelings, and it ended his chances of being friends with her. He thought he did learn something from that experience. In the future he would think twice, before acting so quickly. Then suddenly, his thoughts came back to Joe's story about the girl at the swimming pool. Certainly, by acting quickly, Joe had obviously taken advantage of the opportunity presented to him; or did he? Possibly! Maybe he would have to reconsider his logic. It was strangely different about Joe, because he was always so quiet, reserved and serious most of the time. 'Oh well, it'll happen to me when it's time for it to happen.' He thought to himself.

For now he was content being here with his friends, in this wonderful place. It was like living in paradise. There was the beauty of nature every where. There were wide open spaces with clear air and clean water, and it was free for him and all the boys to enjoy. Greg had long sense become aware of his unique opportunity, and how lucky he was to be living in such a beautiful place. He was very happy now to have learned so much already, and he knew there was going to be so much more to learn. He was going-to be involved with building the boat, and the ramp on which to keep it. He would be going out in the Gulf of Mexico, to fish and to explore the open waters. Best of all, he would have these great friends with which to share all these new experiences. He could hardly believe how lucky he was to have joined this particular Boy Scout troop. If he had not joined this troop, he would not have met Skipper. If he had not met the Skipper, he would be back in Tampa, living his life with his mother and her husband. He would be alone and bored, and he would be trying to find some way to entertain himself all day, while his parents were at work. Yes! He was definitely very lucky, so far, he thought.

CHAPTER 26

PATERNAL AND PERSONAL REFLECTIONS

WHEN HE LIVED AT home, he learned he could never count on his father. Even i f he said he was going to pick Greg up, and take him some where for the afternoon to spend some time together, that meant nothing in reality. There were many times his father never showed up at the scheduled time. Greg soon learned to have something on hand to read or to entertain himself with when his father scheduled an afternoon with him. It was also usual when he did spend the afternoon with his father, that they would go to some bar familiar to his father, where it had been pre arranged that his father could hook up with some of his favorite drinking buddies. Greg soon became friendly and familiar enough with most of them to be on a first name basis. He spent much of the time with his father, in bars playing shuffle board, or pin ball machines, while his father socialized. During this time he learned to never allow himself to become disappointed if his father was a few hours late, or a few days late. Eventually, he learned it was common for him not to show up at all, and never offer an excuse. This was how his father's life was now. It was how he chose to live. Most of his fathers friends also embodied a similar lifestyle.

One of the best things about having so much time to himself Greg learned, was that the privacy it afforded him gave him plenty of time in which to read the library books he carefully chose. He chose them with the help of the librarian, with whom he had become friends. She became familiar to him because of the many hours he spent there.

He also had plenty of time to indulge in his private intimate, fantasy world. It was here during these times, while exercising his stimulating and vivid imagination that he remembered some of the different and arousing dreams from his earlier years. They crept into and intertwined with his thoughts many times during the day, and often when he least expected it.

Ever since he left Georgia, he had experienced more frequent episodes of these types of thoughts intruding into his stream of consciousness.

This had been true except for the sixth grade year, when he was at the catholic boarding school. He did not remember ever having any erotic thoughts, fantasies, or stimulating dreams while there. Clearly that was changing now. Ever since he had learned from his Georgia cousins that they indulged in what they called, "self-stim", he could be awakened by a sudden messy dream. It would awaken him from his sleep. He never woke up in time to keep from making a warm wet spot in his underwear or on the bare sheets. Then he would have to put up with the cold moist spot for the rest of the night. On most occasions he would simply squirm around and maneuver himself away from it, and then slowly and contentedly drift off back to sleep. There were times, during long days when he was alone, that he could have two or more sessions a day. He found it was easier and quicker to complete a session; If he had any kind of extra mental participation aid, such as a book with certain types of special scenes, or pictures of attractive, scantily clad women.

It was interesting he remembered, that the night Joe told the boys about the swimming pool experience, and after all the other boys climbed into their beds for sleep, he was the first one to have his bed become still and quiet. He did have the help of his vividly imagined images that his mind conjured from the incomplete tale Joe told. He would use the incompletely imagined images of the girl, and their friend Joe being together, many times in the future. It was now stored in his memory banks. He would definitely use it many more times in the future, he thought.

CHAPTER 27

SKIPPER THOUGHTS

LATER THAT NIGHT, WHILE lying in his cot, when every one else was asleep, Greg started thinking about Skipper, and then those thoughts kept expanding. Greg thought about how meeting Skipper had changed his life for so much the better, and in so many different ways. When Skipper was around he was always teaching all the other boys, and Greg in particular, about one thing or another, and often many things. It was as if he had to be teaching. He seemed to take immense pleasure in sharing his knowledge. One of the many things Skipper made Greg promise him was that he would never smoke a cigarette before he was eighteen. Because of his love and respect for Skipper, Greg promised, and he intended on keeping that promise. He realized Skipper only wanted the best for all of his troop members, and he was happy that included him.

Skipper was always talking about how important it was to get an education. He pointed out and stressed to Greg, and the other boys that they should always take advantage of any elective educational courses offered in the public schools. These courses were free now, but later on, after high school, a similar educational course would cost big money. There were several courses available now, he pointed out such as an elective in Latin, and an advanced English course, but later on when they were in high school, there would be many more different and exciting types of electives offered. Skipper believed Greg should take all the mathematics electives, such as algebra, geometry and trigonometry that his high school offered. There would also be chemistry, physics and biology courses he could take, that were in addition to the required subjects. Even if Greg had no intention of pursuing a higher education after high school, the knowledge he could acquire for free, would always be helpful for whatever Greg wanted to do later in life. Skipper continually stressed how important it was to learn to read, not just to read like every one else, but to read faster than any one else, and with increased comprehension. He said this rapid reading with increased comprehension was one of the most important skills a young person could acquire. The important thing was to practice every day, just like a sporting activity, where practice daily made you get better at it.

Greg wasn't always sure, just exactly what Skipper was talking about all of the time. He did believe the significance of it was going to become more clear as time passed. He also was becoming aware of the fact that much of what Skipper talked about was slowly but surely taking root and then growing in his own brain. Week by week, month by month his awareness of the importance of the things Skipper was telling him, continued to grow, and enlarge and become a bigger part of him. He was also aware that it was by the repetition of certain subjects, that the whole picture became more clear over time. He could not help but wonder how much awareness he would have of these important life issues, if it were not for the Skipper caring enough to teach him. His mother, father and step father never seemed to have time to talk about such things. Skipper somehow made and found the time to talk with the boys about the things they wanted to talk about.

PART 3

CHAPTER 28

AN ACCIDENT

When the boys got back to the ranch later that morning, they and Skipper unloaded the lumber and supplies from the big truck he had rented. They had to be ready to go in to town early the next morning to get the special plywood for the boat. Over a late dinner that night, they told Skipper and the Parkers about their trips to the boat house. How they had cut and loaded the tree segments, how they used the system of pulleys, and how they unloaded and stacked the logs in the front yard. They told them about the beautiful spring, all the fish they had seen, and the size of the gar in the under water grotto in front of the house. Each boy in his own way, excitedly told them how much they liked it at the beach house. They got even more animated talking about how great it would be when they had a boat with which to go exploring beyond the bend in the bayou. They were eager to see what the rest of the bayou was like, and how far away the entrance to the gulf was from the house. They just knew the fishing was always going to be good, and they would always be able to catch their dinners, and have fresh fish any time they wanted. It would be just like here at the ranch, where they always had their own private fishing lake. It was a similar kind of a special place, one where they could always catch fish any time they wanted. Except that, at the Hudson house it would be salt water fish in stead of fresh water fish. They talked excitedly about the variety of fish, and how many fish there were, right in front of the house. The boys had seen all of this when they went swimming and snorkeling. When they finally slowed down in their descriptions and excitement for a moment, Skipper said,

"I've read some where that those bigger fish you saw may be a type of Alligator Gar. They can get up to three hundred pounds in weight, and up to ten feet long. There have even been some unsubstantiated reports of larger ones attacking men. I don't know if it is true, but I think we should all be a little cautious when they're around. I would say to always keep your eyes on them."

"Yeah, that makes sense. We were a little nervous when we first saw them, but they didn't seem interested in us." Joe said.

"Maybe we should get some spear guns to have at the house." Tommy said.

"I've used them before." said Matt. "I used to go spear fishing with my cousins, it was off of the Courtney Campbell Causeway, at the first bridge. We never saw any thing as big as these gar, but I bet a powerful spear gun would take care of them." he added with his signature sniff, and a satisfied smile.

"We can consider it, but first I want to see them for myself. I'll do it with you one of the next times we're over there." said Skipper.

"Now, we better get a good nights sleep. We have a really big day in front us tomorrow. We'll want to get an early start with all we have to do. Will you please fix us one of your extra special breakfasts in the morning, Mrs. Parker?"

The next morning they were up early, and had a delicious, filling breakfast of bacon and eggs, pancakes and country fried potatoes, After breakfast was finished, they got an early start heading to the Mac Dill air force base. Skipper drove the truck. Joe sat in front with Skipper. Tommy, Matt and Greg rode in the back of the truck. The truck bed had high wooden slats for the side walls. They were a foot higher than the cab roof. At one point later in the trip, Matt climbed up on to the railing in back of the cab. He wanted to look around and see where they were. Then he decided that he preferred staying up there. The view was much better, and the breeze felt good on his face. He sat on the railing on the right side of the cab, facing forward, with his feet resting on the top of the roof of the cab.

"Hey! It feels good up here. I like this feeling of the wind in my face." Matt said.

"I don't think Skipper wants you up there Matt." said Tommy.

"I don't think it's a good idea either." said Greg.

"I'll be O.K.! I can hold on to the railing right here." Matt said.

"I don't think it's a good idea." said Tommy.

"Hey! Tommy, I'm fine up here. OK?" said Matt, with a definitive sniff.

Every thing was fine for a long while, but that changed abruptly. As their truck approached a busy cross roads on the out skirts of town, a car coming from the right side was going too fast to stop, and with the brakes-locked, and the tires squealing loudly, it slid out into the cross road; and when it stopped, it was straight in front of them. The Skipper had to slam the breaks on hard, and swerve to the left, trying not to hit the car which was now stopped directly in front of them. Greg could feel the sudden deceleration, and the swerve to the left. He tried to brace himself and reach for Tommy at the same time. They were both thrown down on to the floor, and up against the forward bulkhead. When they stopped, both boys stood up, and it was then that they saw that Matt was not sitting on the top of the truck any more. Greg and Tommy quickly climbed up on the railing, and looked down in front of the truck. They could see Matt's crumpled body on the ground, he was on the right side of the front of the truck. Matt was lying on his right side, and he was not moving. Greg started to yell to Skipper, to tell him what had happened. Then he could see that Joe and Skipper were scrambling to get out of the truck. Joe had seen Matt's body fly over him. He watched in startled horror as Matt's body struck the hood of the truck, right in front of of his eyes, and then disappear as he bounced off the hood, and on to the ground in front of the truck. He yelled out to Skipper as he saw Matt's body fly on to the hood, and then off again, and on to the ground in front of the truck.

Matt had not regained consciousness by the time the ambulance arrived. He did not appear to have any broken bones, as there was no exaggerated angulations of his extremities. He had deep abrasions on the left side of his body and face from when he landed on the rough road surface. He had obviously bounced and flipped over on to his right side. He had a deep abrasion on the left side of his face, and a large swatch of scalp hair was missing. He was unconscious and totally unresponsive. He was as limp as a rag doll. Greg did not remember ever seeing any one in this kind of condition before. It was an awful feeling seeing Matt, looking dead like that. Then he remembered, he had once seen a dead black man. He was lying on the ground, face up, in front of his apartment in colored town. He had been stabbed in the back of the neck with an ice pick, by his wife. She was obviously still very upset about something; as she was still trying to kick him in his unresponsive face, repeatedly. He didn't move either, he looked just like Matt looked now.

Skipper rode in the ambulance with Matt to the hospital. Joe drove the truck to the hospital. They all waited in the hospital waiting room until Matt's parents arrived. Tommy and Greg told the police and Matt's parents what they had seen happen. They told them, that Tommy and Greg had both warned Matt not to be sitting on top of the truck like that, but he had ignored their warnings. There was no way for Skipper and Joe to know that Matt was sitting on top of the cab, or they would have certainly stopped the truck and made him get down. Greg and Tommy both expressed how bad they felt; they were sorry they had not done more to prevent the accident from happening. They explained that at the time, they both felt like it would have been a mistake for them to physically try to make Matt get down while the truck was underway. Matt had stubbornly refused their friendly suggestions. They thought that if they had tried to make him get down while the truck was moving, bad things could have happened. But, now here was Matt, unconscious, and in the hospital, so they must have made the wrong decision in not making him come down. In discussing the various options with Matt's parents and Skipper, it was obvious the boys were very distraught. Matt's parents could see what their dilemma had been, and they could tell how badly the boys now obviously felt. Before they left the hospital, Matt's parents did their best to convince Tommy and Greg they did not blame them for what happened. They all finally agreed, that the best course of action would have been for them to signal Skipper, in some way, and make him aware of the situation.

By the time they left the hospital, Matt had not recovered consciousness. Skipper and the three boys went on to the air force base and collected the plywood. Before they drove back to the ranch, they checked with the hospital again. Matt was still unconscious, but was other wise doing satisfactory. His vital signs were stable, and the other injuries were considered minor, in comparison with the deep, unresponsive coma he was in.

It was not until the sixth day in the early afternoon, that he started to respond to painful stimuli. On the tenth day after the accident, Matt woke up. He sat up, and looked around blankly for several minutes. He was obviously completely lost, and totally confused about why and where he was. When he recognized his parents, he asked them why he was in the hospital. He had no memory of the event. It wasn't until the following week that he remembered he had been on the way to get plywood for the boat; and that he was with Skipper and the other boys. He then started remembering more and more details. He finally remembered that they were all going to start building a boat together. His next question was when could he go back to the ranch, and join in on the boat building project. His parents were not sure at first if they would ever let him go back to the ranch. After all, they had almost lost him, while he was in Skippers care. After a week of Matt begging, pleading, and then crying with his parents, they relented, and said, if and when the doctor said it was safe, they would allow him to try it. They made it stringently clear, that Matt had to exercise better judgment in the future, and if they ever heard anything to the contrary, they would insist he come home immediately.

CHAPTER 29

MATT RETURNS

IT WAS THREE WEEKS after the accident when Matt returned to the ranch. Greg and the other boys thought that there was something not quite the same about Matt, from that time forward. Greg probably knew Matt better than the other boys since they were the same age, and because of this, had spent more time together. They had shared some secrets, and personal thoughts with each other, more so than with the other boys. The doctors had given instructions that Matt was not to engage in strenuous activities. No heavy lifting. No straining. No long hours of work without rest. Every one at the ranch understood these limitations, and the rational for them. For this reason, Matt was watched over by the adults, and protected from the more strenuous work projects by every one. He became relegated to more of a 'fetch it' designation. Initially they all joked and laughed about the light duty status. They would say things like, "Boy, I need to get conked on the head, then I could get the easy jobs."

As the days passed, and progress on the boat moved along smoothly and to every ones satisfaction, Matt's attitude about the way the others were required to treat him changed. The joking around seemed to irritate him, increasingly more as the days went by. Greg did not think any of the other boys, and certainly not the Skipper, minded that Matt was not allowed to do as much work as them selves on the boat construction, or on the ramp at the boat house. In all other endeavors Matt was certainly treated as equally as any of the others.

When Greg eventually tried talking with Matt, like they did before the accident, about their secrets, and other personal things, it was as if Matt was not completely engaged in the conversation, he seemed distant, and not willing to talk. It seemed strange to Greg, and he did not know what to make of the way Matt thought and felt about things now. It was a different Matt. Greg did mention his observations to Skipper, but the consensus was to just let some time pass, and to continue to treat him like always, except for the restrictions placed on him by his doctors. At first these were subtle things that Greg noticed and felt, but never the less he believed there was something fundamentally different about Matt. It was mostly in his attitude about and towards the other boys, that these changes were noted the most.

CHAPTER 30

RANCH TIME

IN THE MIDDLE OF the summer, they got a row boat. It was like the one at their lake in the swamp, and they kept it in the front yard of the boat house. On days off from the construction projects, or after work was over for the day, they took the boat out in to the open waters of the bayou, and explored the inlet that opened to the Gulf of Mexico. Half way to the gulf entrance, they passed a peninsula of land on the left hand side of the bayou that had several modern houses constructed along the shores. On some occasions they saw attractive young girls in the front yard of one of the houses. The girls appeared to be about their age, maybe a little older. They were always in shorts, or in bathing suits. They were too attractive not to look at. So the boys all looked at the girls, trying not to be too obvious, as they rowed by in their boat. It was not long before Joe and Tommy started saying things like. "We have got to get over there one of these days, and talk to those girls."

"Yeah, and when we get the big boat over here, maybe we can take them out fishing with us." Greg said.

The construction of the boat was progressing faster than had been expected. When they were not actively working on the boat, the boys enjoyed the opportunities the ranch and the boat house offered. Greg and Tommy had both bought BB gun rifles. They looked just like the rifles in the western movies. Greg practiced shooting at every opportunity. He discovered that by practicing, he was slowly becoming a better shot. Tommy was a very good shot from the beginning. He rarely missed. One of their favorite past times was to hang out under the thick grove of oak trees; in the front of the property, on the high side and closer to the paved road. Here, there were numerous and different birds flittering among the branches. When they wanted something different for dinner, they would kill a half dozen blue jays and mocking birds. They became good at removing the feathers and cleaning out the intestines, leaving the bird in tact. They cooked their birds whole, well floured, in a covered, oiled skillet. They sometimes got lucky and shot a few dove when they went hunting. The boys could not really tell a big difference in taste between the song birds and the dove when they ate them. But Lindsey and Mrs. Parker said the dove were better, and preferred them.

One of their big surprises, was discovering how good a shot Lindsey was. They somehow did not expect a one armed man would be so good with a rifle. He did use a tree limb or some other prop for a barrel support, but he was deadly accurate. If he was shooting a 22 rifle, he could hit the bird in the head every time, and not mess up the meat like they frequently did. Greg, Tommy and Matt always tried to do the same thing, but found out it was not as easy as it looked when Lindsey did it.

Greg also discovered, during this time, that he liked to take long walks around the property by himself. He would usually take a path that led him near to where they had pulled the dead calf out of the cow his first night at the ranch. That unforgettable experience had happened on his very first trip to the ranch. He liked to lie on his back in the grass, and watch the clouds drift lazily by overhead. He could let his mind drift, just like the clouds. He always wondered if God was watching him now, while he was lying there, and thinking about God. His scapular had long ago worn out. He had sown it back together several times, but finally there was not much of it left to sew back together. He did not go to the Catholic Church in down town Tampa, now that he spent so much of his time at the ranch and the boat house. He was almost always at the ranch on Sundays, and he did not know of any one with a connection who could get him another scapular. He thought that he could probably find some one if he looked hard enough.

As he continued to think about his scapular problem, he came to realize that this process of thinking things through, had brought him face to face with a new reality. None of the other boys he knew wore a scapular, and they seemed to get along fine without it. It was still on his mind periodically, and that made him uncomfortable. He knew and believed deeply, that if he died without it being around his neck, he might not get the direct pass in to heaven like he had been taught. This led him to make a major decision. He decided he would beat the odds of getting into heaven another way. It was astounding to him now that the answer was so very clear and easy; he would simply be a good enough person for God, that he would get into heaven without wearing the scapular. That decision made him feel much better about his ultimate fate. He was still having feelings of guilt, from time to time, for his bad behavior that summer in California, and at the boarding school. He prayed that God had forgiven him for that. From now on, he decided, he would never have to worry about going to hell again. And all he had to do was be the best person he could be, at all times. It was such a wonderful realization at how simple it was all going to be from now on.

While lying on his back and feeling the warmth of the ground on his back, watching the clouds drift lazily by, he thought about how happy he was now that he had solved the problem of not going to hell. He then came to the realization that he was also more happy ever since being here at the ranch, than he had ever been before. Well, maybe some of the times he spent in Georgia, with his Aunt Lou and his cousins, that was good too. It was, however, definitely second best. In both places he could go bare foot, roam through the woods exploring nature and the wilderness, go fishing and imagine to himself, that even Huckleberry Finn would be jealous.

CHAPTER 31

TIME WITH SKIPPER

GREG ALSO THOUGHT ABOUT Skipper a lot. He knew he would not be here, if it were not for the fact that Skipper liked him. He remembered one day especially, when just he and Skipper were alone. They were driving over to the boat house to join Joe, Tommy and Matt who were putting the finishing touches to the preparations on the ramp. The logs had been in position, and the rails had been securely attached for the past two weeks. They were working on a pulley system that would pull the boat out of the water, and up the rails. They were also working on a way to secure the boat to the top of the ramp. Skipper spoke first, and started the conversation.

"I think you should know Greg, I believe you're a special person."

"Why do you say that, Skipper?" asked Greg.

"To start with you are a good person, you are naturally kind to everyone. You don't pick fights. You do your work willingly, and you don't complain about things. You are easy to be around, and to have around, not every one is like that"

"I haven't always been so good." said Greg, thinking about his year in California.

"Maybe not, but you are now, and that's what counts. The past is the past. We should not live in the past, and we do not live in the future. We live in the present. Saying that, it suddenly reminds me of a little poem I read somewhere. It is apropos to our discussions. I think It goes like this:

YESTERDAY IS BUT A DREAM
AND TOMORROW IS ONLY A VISION
BUT TODAY WELL LIVED
MAKES EVERY YESTERDAY A DREAM OF HAPPINESS
AND EVERY TOMORROW A VISION OF HOPE
LIVING WELL TODAY IS LIFE'S PATH TO HAPPINESS."

"Wow! That is good Skipper. I need to write it down so I can memorize it." said Greg

"I thought you would appreciate it Greg. You know, I believe you have a vein of gold flowing deeply through you. I also believe life can be a lot like mining for gold. If you don't work hard enough and don't dig deep enough, and keep at it, you might not ever find the gold. I for one believe you have much more gold to be mined. I intend to make sure we mine all that gold in you." Skipper said.

"I try to be the best person I can be Skipper. I want to please God by being as good as God wants us to be." said Greg.

"You know Greg, Joe is not going to be with us after this summer is over.". Greg was surprised by this statement.

"He told us he was going to be here another year, just a short while ago." Greg said.

"I know, that's what he thought, but his father was ordered to be in Texas two months from now, and as much we don't like it, that's how it's going to be. So, with Joe gone, I've decided I am going to put you in charge of the boat. You will be the captain. When we do get it over to Hudson, I will announce to the others that you are going to be the captain. You will be in charge whenever we take her out." said Skipper.

"Wow Skipper! That's a big responsibility. Are you sure I'm ready for that?"

"Yes, it is a big responsibility, but I believe and know you're ready for it. You have shown me the most maturity and growth over the past few months, and I believe you will continue to develop more strongly in that direction. So I think you should be the boat's captain. We'll wait a while to announce it to the others, but you and I will know that it is what is going to be."

"It's fine with me Skipper, if that's what you want. I will certainly do my best to not let you down."

"I know you will Greg. Now come on over here, scoot between my legs, and steer the rest of the way. We've got to get you ready to drive even before you come of age. I know you drive the old ford truck sometime on the property, but that is a big difference from driving on these roads. There are some bad drivers out here. Remember this about driving. Always drive defensively. You don't know anything about that other driver who is coming at you on the other side of the road. Think of them all, as possibly dangerous. So be prepared and drive defensively."

Since the conversation about the boat with Skipper had taken place, Greg had been too excited to think very much about anything else. Now, he really knew, that his life had never been better. Also, he and Skipper had become better friends in a totally different way recently. The two of them had many more private, and sometimes intimate talks. He had already told every one at the ranch he was going to go out for the football team this year.

Skipper told Greg that he did not think it was a good idea, and he was not in favor of it. Skipper was not a big fan of football. When he was in high school, he played football, he said. He had a very good friend, his best friend at the time. They played side by side in the front line. His friend played the tackle position and Skipper played guard, they played right next to each other. On the last day Skipper ever played football, his team was winning the game by two touch downs. The other team had the ball. He and his friend thought they had read the next play. They both believed the half back was coming through on their side with the ball. When they bent over, and waited for the ball to be hiked, his friend looked quickly at Skipper and winked. He had a knowing smile on his lips.

The half back took the hand off from the quarter back, circled around, picked up speed and came straight at the two of them, as he approached, he lowered his head and crashed full into his friend who also had his head down. The collision caused his friend's neck to be broken on that play. He never walked again. He was a quadriplegic the remainder of his life, which was not very long after the accident. Skipper, never played football again. He never recommended that any one play football. He did not believe anyone should risk their health, their brain or their life, for a game, and a few moments of soon to be forgotten glory.

His mother also was not happy about his decision. They both thought he was too small to be playing football this year. Greg was adamant about it. He wanted to try out for the team. He had never played any serious team sports, and he felt like he needed to know if he could. When Skipper asked Greg what position he wanted to play, it was obvious Greg had not even thought about this yet. His answer was,

"I'll show up at practice, and see what the coach thinks is best for me."

One night, at the ranch, a week later, he was talking with Skipper in the big bed. Matt and Tommy were already asleep on the cots. Earlier they had all been talking and laughing at a joke Matt heard at school. Just before Greg was about to go to sleep, Skipper said to him,

"Slide over here next to me, and let's talk a bit. After Greg squirmed his way over next to him, Skipper said,

"Have you ever worn a jock strap? You know, you will have to wear one when you play football?"

"No, I have never put one on. Is there a trick to it, or do you just put it on." Greg answered.

"Yes, there is a trick to it. Do you want me to show you how to put it on?" Skipper asked.

"Yes, please show me." Greg said.

"The purpose of the jock strap is to protect your testicles from getting injured, when you have physical contact with another player. What I have always been taught, is to push your testicles up in to the inguinal canal, which is just above the scrotum. You do it on both sides. Then you use the jock strap to keep them up in the right position." said Skipper.

"I don't I know what you mean." said Greg.

"Do you want me to show you how to do it? It's very simple, once you know how?" said Skipper.

"Yes, please." said Greg.

"Take down the sheet, so you can see what I'm doing. Now watch me, you take the right testicle like this, and push it up and into this place in the inguinal canal, right here. Like this." said Skipper.

Greg could feel a strange sensation as his testicle slid up into the inguinal canal. When Skipper did the other side, Greg felt the same strange sensation.

"Now, you reach down, and feel your scrotum." said Skipper.

When Greg felt his own scrotum, he could not feel his testicles.

"Hey, They're gone! Where are they? Are they lost?" asked Greg.

"No, No, they're right here." Skipper chuckled. He released his fingers, and Greg could feel the sliding action as they slipped back down in to his scrotum. At the same time Greg suddenly realized that all the manipulations had caused him to start getting an erection.

"Oh, Oh, it getting hard." he said looking at Skipper, sheepishly.

"Oh, that's normal, don't worry about it, but that was a quick response. Are you that quick to get an erection all the time?" asked Skipper.

"Oh Yeah, and it can be a darned nuisance some of the time. It can really be a problem when I'm at school." said Greg.

"Why is that?" Skipper asked.

"It always happens at the worst times. It happens to me several times a day, all during the school day. I never know when it's going to happen. What causes me the most trouble is when the teacher calls me to the front of the class room for some reason. There I am with this hard thing sticking out in front of my pants. So I panic, and I get embarrassed, and I think I can't just walk up in front of the class with me being obvious."

"What do you do?" asked Skipper.

"I usually pretend to have a problem with getting out of my seat. I struggle with the desk, tripping, trying to delay standing up. Then I act like I've got a cramp or an injury in my leg, so I bend over and limp up to the front of the room, pretending like I'm favoring my leg, and that hides it some. Usually it starts going down after a few minutes of this play acting."

"That's clever Greg. Good thinking on your feet, but I've always known you were a clever one." said Skipper.

"So what else do you do when you get an erection?", asked Skipper.

"Well, when I'm at school, nothing, just let it go down on it's own. If I'm by myself, I stimulate myself, and that settles it down and takes care of it fast. Some times, but not often, if I'm with some other guys, we have done it together. I mean, usually, we each do our selves. There was one time when I was with a special friend of mine from school; we tried doing it to each other." said Greg.

"How did you like that experience?" asked Skipper.

"I think it was O.K. It was a little more fun than me doing it by myself. It was definitely different having someone else touching me. I mean, it felt different, and yeah, I guess better in some ways." said Greg.

"Before too many more years now you will be able to share those kinds of experiences with some nice girl of you choice." said Skipper.

"Well, Skipper, I can tell you, I feel like I am ready right now for that kind of experience."

CHAPTER 32

TALKING MORE WITH SKIPPER

After that nights conversation, Greg felt like he and Skipper had broken through a communication barrier. He was more comfortable, and felt better able to talk about difficult and typically forbidden subjects. He wanted to learn about things that until now were off limits to him with adults. Greg had never had a relationship with an adult where he could be so open and honest about the things he thought about and said. This was especially true about subjects relating to Greg's personal life, and his intense interest in sexual matters. Most adults Greg associated with, did not really seem to care or have much of an interest in talking with a boy about the kinds of things he thought about, and felt were important. Perhaps they were so busy with work, and so tired after work, they didn't have the time or energy to be interested. Skipper was different that way. He always seemed interested in what Greg thought about things. He always had time to answer Greg's questions, and just as importantly, Skipper actually encouraged Greg to communicate about his thoughts.

For instance, he felt comfortable talking to Skipper about self stimulation. When Greg brought up the question, what did Skipper think God felt about the subject of boys doing this with themselves, Skipper was willing to discuss the subject with Greg until all his questions were answered. In the long discussion that ensued, Skipper said there was something in the bible about it being wrong for a man to cast his seed upon the ground. Skipper's thoughts on the question of how God felt, was that the bible was written and rewritten many times over several centuries by many different men. Some of these men who were doing the writing and rewriting of the bible may have put a little of their own needs and thoughts into the writings. How could anyone ever know that they got it right, just like God said after so many centuries ago. So Skipper thought that it was probable and certainly possible the bible may not actually represent the exact words of God or Jesus.

"In those days, man and the tribes they belonged to always wanted and needed to increase population growth. If a man wasted his seed, which meant, spilling his flow on to the ground, that would mean one less baby could be born. These days we don't call it seed, we call it semen. I'm sure you boys call it many other things, but it is what shoots out the end of the penis when you have an orgasm. That semen is what makes a baby when it meets a woman's eggs, which come from her ovary. So those old guys, who wrote and rewrote the bible, were creating the words of the bible, and they wanted to a make a man feel guilty about having sex by himself, instead of with a woman. They believed they always needed more people for their community. They probably needed more people to help fight off the bad guys from other tribes. They also needed them to plant food, to harvest the crops, and build things. So I think they had their own motives in mind, when they wrote about those kinds of things." said Skipper.

"So, you don't believe there is anything wrong with it?" asked Greg

"No. I don't believe there is any thing wrong with it, at least from God's perspective. I think times have changed, we don't have the same need for more and more people to be born every day, like they did back then. Think of it this way. God must have made having an orgasm feel so good for a reason. If a man is not ready to have children, because he cannot afford to raise and educate them, or if he just doesn't want children at a certain time of his life, would God want that man or boy to never experience such a wonderful pleasure, like an orgasm, never, not for all of his life? After all was it not God who created the orgasm, and made it feel so good? That would be a really cruel and unjust God. Making an experience feel so good, then saying you can never experience it unless you are going to make a baby. Besides that, I cannot even imagine how any harm is done to other persons for an individual to indulge in masturbation. We already have so many people on the planet now that we cannot feed them all. I do not believe God is that cruel and unjust. Do you think he is Greg?" asked Skipper.

"No, I guess not. But some times he does not seem fair. Look at what happened to Matt. He fell off the truck, and it seems like it changed him in some bad way. He is not the same person he was before the accident." said Greg.

"Every one says God works in mysterious ways. We all have to wait and see what he has in mind for Matt." said Skipper.

"What about the catholic priests? They are supposed to deny themselves sex of any kind. Why would they do that to themselves?" asked Greg.

"I don't really know the answer to that question, but I think the priests, are in a totally different category. I believe they think they are supposed to sacrifice themselves for God. By denying them selves, they stay clean like a virgin girl. When they go to heaven they are supposed to be as pure and clean as the day they were born. I think that is how it is supposed to go. I am not a catholic, but that is what I think, and what I understand about the subject." said Skipper.

"Do they really do it? I mean never have any kind of sex?" asked Greg.

"That is a good question. If you read very much history about the Catholic Church, it's difficult to come to that conclusion. Certainly if you follow the news these days, there are too many accusations about them having sex with young boys." said Skipper.

"That doesn't sound like they are actually sacrificing themselves." said Greg.

"No, I have to agree about that. My self, I always remember Ernest Hemingway's short poem.

I KNOW THAT PET CATS SCREW, AND THAT MONKS MASTURBATE AT NIGHT, BUT, WHAT CAN I DO TO MAKE THINGS RIGHT.

He was a catholic, and maybe he just was exercising poetic license about monks masturbating at night; maybe they do, and maybe they don't. But, that helps me keep it all in perspective. Now that I brought up his name, let me tell you something I recently heard about him. The news is out that he has just completed a short novel that is supposed to be very good. I think it is something about an old man catching a giant marlin off the coast of Cuba. Since you love fishing so much, It should be right down your alley." said Skipper.

"Hey Skipper, I've heard about it at school. They're going to have us read it this year for English class." said Greg.

"Isn't that a coincidence I will be very interested to hear what you think about It." said Skipper.

CHAPTER 33

GIRLS AND OTHER THINGS

Another time, later in their relationship, when they were again talking privately, Greg wanted to ask Skipper what his thoughts were about girls and women.

"Skipper, will you tell me about girls and what they are like. And, I want to know more about their, you know, their private parts. The other boys are always talking about them, and how special they are. I don't even know what they look like, or what makes them so different from the boys? I'm embarrassed to be so ignorant in front of the other guys."

"Oh boy!" said Skipper. "You've asked a tough one this time. I'll tell you what I know about private parts. That part of your question is easy, because it's only anatomy. Telling you what girls and women are like is another story. That verges on the mythical, the philosophical, and the unknowable. So let's do the easy part first.

First, the word p—y is just a slang term. It is used to describe the parts of a woman's anatomy between her legs. Where the penis and scrotum is on a boy, is where a female has her external genitalia. All of a woman's external genitalia, is what the guys call a p—y. I don't know exactly why they call it that, or how long it has been called that, but it's here to stay, I'm sure of that. Anyway, a girl's private parts have these, they are like lips, and they are on each side of the vagina. The vagina is the actual cavity or passage that goes up inside the woman, it's in front of the anus, and connects to the uterus. The uterus is where the baby develops, but it is not really a part of the p—y. ; that is the part of a woman that guys can feel when they touch them down there between the legs. The vagina is also where they stick their fingers into them, and is also where a man puts his penis when a man and a woman want to make a baby, or just make love. That's what some guys call, fingering it. I guess it's because it is so warm, soft and furry, that they call it a kitten name, but I don't really know. It certainly doesn't purr like a cat. But, it can fart, or at least make a farting sound." said Skipper.

"Farting p—y! That doesn't sound like something good." said Greg, with a nervous laugh.

"Maybe not, but I can tell you this, when and if you do hear a pussy fart, you won't care one bit." said Skipper.

"Why is that Skipper?"

"Because you will have some part of you, either your penis or your fingers inside of the vagina and when you are playing with it, a little farting sound is the last thing you care about. Besides those kind of farts do not stink." said Skipper

"To go on, the reason it is considered so great to the guys, is because when you put your penis into the vagina, it's warm and slippery, and it feels really nice. Each and every woman's thing, has a mind of it's own. Maybe that's another reason why they call it a cat name. You never know what an owner of one of them will do next, so there is always that unique element of surprise. That's what makes each one of them so exciting and so different from woman to woman. Another thing, It's totally different from masturbation. There you have to create all the movements and sensations by yourself, using your own imagination to create a fantasy. When you're with a woman the two of you together create a real life fantasy. You do this by making many different kinds of movements, and those different movements can create different sensations. So you do not need to create a fantasy in your own mind. The two of you create it together. Any woman you're with, can have a totally different attitude about their private parts, at any given time. You can never expect it to be the same attitude, not in the same woman at any given time, and certainly not in different women.

Now here is the important part for you to remember. Some women like to use theirs for pleasure; theirs and yours. Then there are some women who like to use theirs as a means to punish or hurt a man. They can do that by getting a man to liking it too much, and then they with hold it from him. They punish him by not letting him have it whenever he wants it. Some women do like to give a man and themselves pleasure. If you ever find a woman, like that, who enjoys being erotic, and giving pleasure to herself and to you, then you have an opportunity for a wonderful experience and relationship.

On the other hand, there are some women who do not enjoy giving pleasure, not to you, not themselves, nor anyone else. If you run into one like that, my advice would be to get out of that relationship as quickly and painlessly as possible. That's my advice. There are many reasons for these differences in a woman's attitude about sharing, but the point is, if they don't like it, you probably won't either, certainly not in the long run. This difference in attitude a woman has about herself, is what makes the experience so different from woman to woman.

Those lips I mentioned earlier, they can also be totally different. Some times they're long and floppy, and sometimes they're almost non existent. So each and everyone has it's own unique beauty. This difference in the appearance of the lips, and the attitude the woman has towards sharing, is what can make each experience so unique and different from woman to woman. It won't be too much longer before you will be able to start finding out for your self. The very fact that you're asking so many questions now means you are growing up. Your hormones are beginning to surge, and it is time for you to begin thinking about these kinds of things. You are becoming aware, and you are ready to find out. So it won't be long. You just have to be patient a little longer. Your time will come." said Skipper.

"I hope you're right Skipper. I know I think about this stuff a lot. I know my time will eventually come, but when is my question. It cannot be any too soon as far as I am concerned.

"Now Greg, I'll tell you the most important things for you to know about girls and women, for now and for ever." said Skipper.

"What's that?" asked Greg.

"As long as you are a single man, never, ever, put your penis into a woman without first putting on a condom, a rubber. If you do, you risk two things that can ruin your life forever. And I do mean forever. Right now, I'm talking about the while you're alive kind of forever, not the heaven and hell kind of forever, when you are dead. The only reason not to put on a rubber is if you are with your wife, or if you are planning to create a baby. If that is what you want, and you are planning to have a baby that you WANT to take care of for the rest of its life, then you do not need to use a rubber."

"Why is that?" asked Greg.

"Good, you're paying attention, that's the right question. First, you can get a girl pregnant. To have a baby before you're ready to raise it, take care of it, and educate it, is one of the worst things a person can do, in my opinion. That's what I believe! We already have too many unwanted children on the planet. When there is a lack of family unity and love, where the mother and the father want to raise a child together, that is why some young people look for other groups of people, like gangs, to substitute for their family. The second thing is, you risk catching a venereal disease, and that can also ruin your life for ever. You should promise me now, like you did about smoking, that you won't have sex with a girl, without using a condom."

"Sure Skipper, of course I promise. It makes sense the way you talk about it." said Greg.

"Let me warn you. It is not going to be as easy as it sounds right now, making that promise. Because when the opportunity presents itself, and you're all hot and bothered, and if you don't have a condom with you, it can be hard to say no. So as we say in the scouts, be prepared." said Skipper, smiling.

"Skipper, how come you never got married, and have some children of your own?" asked Greg.

"That's pretty simple." said Skipper. "I haven't found the right woman yet; not so far, anyway. So I let you boys substitute for my family. Having you boys around is a good alternative for me not having my own children. I get to watch you grow up. I get to teach you about important things. I enjoy watching you boys have fun and learn about life. It makes me happy that I have the means to provide that opportunity for all of you."

"Well, I'm sure glad we have you in our lives Skipper." said Greg." Then he added, "I wonder why more parents are not more like you? You're always so willing to talk with us, and explain things to us in different ways, so that we understand."

"I think part of the answer is, I like to teach, and I do have the time. More importantly, as you must know, I make the time, because it is a priority with me. Another reason some men do not make good fathers is the fact that they fail to put on that rubber when they should. They cause a baby to be born when they don't really want it, and they cannot afford it. Those kind of guys frequently resent having a child around, they think of them as ruining their life. In reality they are the ones who could have prevented the pregnancy in the first place. Another big factor is this, even though a man is too selfish and doesn't demonstrate responsibility; many women are also not willing to say no when they should."

"Why do they do that?" asked Greg.

"The simplest answer is they want or need the attention at the moment, or they think they need it, even though it is potentially the wrong kind of attention." said Skipper.

"Now, let's talk about something much more difficult. I'm talking about the other part of your question. What are girls and women really like? Now, that is one of life's greatest mysteries, and there is no easy answer. I can tell you the one thing I do know, man has been seeking the answer to that question, since the beginning of time. Some of the worlds greatest literature has been written about the subject. Starting with the Bible, and why Eve listened to the snake, and ate the apple when she knew she was not supposed to do It. See what I mean? So for many centuries, man has been in a quandary over the subject. Maybe one day you will add your own personal observations to the worlds literature. I will tell you what I think about women in general. They are a mystery wrapped up in an enigma, that can all change in an instant. Just consider Eve eating that "apple", and changing the course of mankind forever. That mystery alone should give you something to think about for a while.

Now, I'll tell you another thing I believe strongly."

"What's that Skipper?"

"Learning to read and write well, is one of the most important skills there is for a boy to learn. I hope for your sake, that you do learn to love it and enjoy it. It can become a great passion, and a life long activity. Like reading which you already enjoy, writing and reading can become your best friends for life. They can keep you busy, happy and always with something to do, that comes from inside of your self, while others are bored, trying to find some external means, outside of themselves, to find entertainment, or just spend their time. It also provides an opportunity to be creative, and being creative can be one of the most rewarding activities I can think of.

"Why is that Skipper?"

"I think being creative is the ultimate realization of man's potential. It causes the brain to stretch, grow and expand. The rewards of being successfully creative are a unique source of enjoyment. Consider Leonardo Da Vinci, Michael Angelo, and even Ernest Hemingway, and the mark they have made on civilization. That is what I am talking about. But, this talk is getting way too serious for this late at night. That should be enough serious discussions for one night, now slide on over here, and let's get some sleep." said Skipper.

CHAPTER 34

SPORTS

WHEN FOOTBALL SEASON BEGAN, Greg was excited. He showed up for the first day of practice early. He soon discovered to his dismay, that he did not have a great talent for throwing or catching the ball. He was as good as some of the guys, but it was clear to him from the beginning, he was not going to be a quarterback, a half back, nor a receiver. He found the football did not stick to his fingers when he tried to catch it. It seemed like some of the guys had glue on their hands, the way they could catch the ball from almost any position, even while running at full speed down the field. He discovered that running, and trying to catch the ball at the same time was not one of his talents either. That left only the defensive team positions open for him. He was not fast enough for the open field positions. He tried to play the tackle position, but it was obvious to all, he was like a tiny midget compared to some of the other guys standing in line beside him. He managed to make a few decent tackles, but he always paid a big price, sustaining injuries with each tackle.

After several days, the coach took him aside and suggested quietly and nicely, that he should consider another sport for this year. The coach said, maybe in the next year or two he might grow more and become big enough. If he did grow, he might become big enough to play, but for this year, due to his size, he should forget it.

Greg was truly disappointed, but he knew he must go forward, and face the unhappiness he felt head on. He could not change the fact of his size being too small to play football this year, but it made it more acceptable to him that both Skipper and his mother were openly pleased when he told them he was not going to be playing football this year.

Every sport he attempted that year turned out the same way. In track he simply was not fast enough to make the team. He found that for him the high jump was too high, and the broad jump was too broad. The hurtles were fun, and he liked to jump over them while running fast, but they were not his special talent either. He tried each of the different track and field sports events. The results were always the same. He was not a good enough athlete to play on any of the team sports. He faced these realities as bravely as he could. Swimming was the only sport in which he may have been good enough to be on the team, he thought, but there was no swimming team, and there would not be until high school. He had to face it, there were no sports in which he could make the team. It was all a big disappointment, but Greg realized he was not the only boy who would not be participating in the schools athletic events. That fact made his disappointment more acceptable, and made it easier for him move forward, and do the things he could do well.

CHAPTER 35

THOUGHTS OF LIFE

ONE DAY GREG WAS lying in the warm grass. He was on his back. He was at his favorite spot on the ranch for privacy. He was watching the high clouds drifting overhead, and thinking. He thought of thanking God for the fact that he had the ranch activities, the boat house projects, and Skipper in his life. For many lazy moments Greg's thoughts drifted along happily, and then suddenly a terrible ugly thought intruded into his happiness. What if something bad happened to Skipper? His wonderful, happy and busy life could be over. Then what would he do? He suddenly dreaded the thought of having to resume living his life, like it had been before he became a scout, and had met Skipper. He remembered the boredom and the loneliness, and the lack of friends. He had no transportation modes available except for his feet, and the public busses. He remembered how that had all changed when he met Skipper and the Parkers. Greg quickly pushed these unpleasant thoughts from his mind. He focused on the reality of his present good life. He did have Skipper, the Parkers, the ranch and the boat house. He also knew that he was going to be captain of the boat when it was finished, and that made his disappointment about sports easier to live with.

The things he did at the ranch were always appreciated, and he liked being there more than any other place he could think of. He was grateful that his mother was so busy with her work, and her husband, that she did not interfere with his being at the ranch. He really enjoyed spending his time with the other scouts. Greg remembered his earlier life, before boarding school, and then again in the fifth grade, his mother did not always make fair decisions about what he was allowed to do. This was especially true if she drank too much. She would suddenly forbid him to go to a birthday party for one of his friends. She would use excuses like, "You don't have a present. You are not going, so forget it." These seemed like such unreasonable and unfair decisions to Greg. She was not usually like that unless she was drinking.

His good fortune of being invited to participate at the ranch activities seemed to work out for his mother as well as himself. Their relationship when he was home had improved significantly. Greg made every effort to make sure it stayed that way. Over the two years she made a couple of trips to the ranch, and the boat house. She wanted to see where and how he spent so much of his time. She only knew he was happy, and he was better behaved now than ever before. When he was home he did his house hold chores without being asked. His school grades were good. His manners and behavior were exemplary. She could only assume that for some reason his change for the better must be related to his joining the scouts, and his time at the ranch. Her few visits to the ranch always went well. She was always invited to eat lunch or dinner by the Parkers. She was obviously satisfied with what she learned about how well they all lived and worked together.

On one different occasion, Greg planed and arranged for Skipper to join his mother, and himself for an afternoon at the causeway. She liked to spend time there when she was not working. It was Greg's secret hope that maybe they would become attracted to one another. After all, his mother was still an attractive woman. It was rare for Greg to see a movie star that was prettier than his mother. It was not so much that he disliked his stepfather, but that he liked Skipper so much more.

Greg and his stepfather had never been close. They're relationship was made much worse by his mother one night, early in their life together. His stepfather had punished him rather severely one day. Greg remembered that when his mother got home, and after having a couple of beers, she became unreasonably upset and angry at his stepfather for his actions. She was so angry that she unwisely forbid him to ever reprimand Greg again in such a manner. He never did, but he and Greg were never close again after that. The two of them never did things together unless his mother was involved. They were cordial and civil to each other, but they never shared the days events, nor had any type of discussions.

Because of this attitude of mutual indifference with his stepfather, Greg believed it would be better for his mother and Skipper to get together. If they did, she would not have to work twelve to fourteen hours a day, six days a week. Greg thought it was becoming clear to him by now, that his stepfather was never going to make enough money to support his mother. She would have to work for the rest of her life. Skipper was a Major in the air force. He obviously made enough money to have a comfortable lifestyle. If they got together, it would be better for his mother and much better for Greg. Greg soon gave up on the idea, when it became clear to him, it was never going to be. He had done his best for her. That was all a boy could do.

CHAPTER 36

CONCERNS

As the school year progressed the boat building project was also nearing completion, but very slowly. The boat was thirty feet long, nine feet wide, and It drew three feet of water. It had a single flat roofed cabin, that extended two-thirds of the way back from the bow. It would be perfect for standing on to fish. It had a thirty horse power gasoline inboard engine, with a three bladed propeller. It was not designed as a speed boat. It was built more along the concept of a trawler. They were going to paint it marine gray, when they got to that phase.

The progress on the boat construction slowed considerably after school started. The week ends and holidays during the school year provided the necessary time to bring it nearer to completion. They hoped they would have it in the water before summer arrived. The boys were all proud of their efforts. The excitement of getting the boat they had helped build over to the boathouse, and loaded on to the railroad tracks was shared by them all. Greg secretly felt the excitement more keenly than the others, knowing that when the time came Skipper would announce to the others he was going to be the captain. He had obtained from the library some books on handling a powerboat, and had been studying diligently in preparation for the day they launched the boat. He studied the right of way rules, anchoring techniques, and managing the boat in heavy weather. He wanted to be prepared when the time came.

They all missed Joe since he had moved to Texas with his parents. He wrote several times, telling them how much he missed them all, and wished he could be there when the boat was launched. Since Joe had been gone, the leadership status among the boys was not as clearly defined. Joe's size, age and maturity of thinking had made him clearly the person in charge. That would have been the situation even if Skipper had not made it clear to all that when Joe was around he was in charge. Tommy was now the oldest of the boys. He was not the natural leader that Joe had been. He did not take charge naturally. He was hesitant to make group decisions quickly, as Joe had done. Because of this feature and aspect of his personality, there was a subtle void of leadership palpable beneath the surface. Greg found out over time, that frequently Tommy would defer to Greg's judgment calls over his own. This was not anything Greg planned, nor advocated. It simply evolved out of the joint recognition of Greg's talent for assuming command, even when he was not trying. Greg had not realized at first that this subtle change in leadership was evolving. It certainly did not create any type of animosity between Tommy and Greg. Greg was aware that when Skipper announced to the others he was appointing Greg to be in charge and captain of the boat when it was launched, he would be elevated in rank automatically. Perhaps Skipper had already assessed the situation, and was acting preemptively.

Matt was still behaving strangely at times. He would sometimes pick a verbal fight with the two of them, even when it was obvious to them, he was in the wrong. This behavior seemed to be a continuation of his resentment of not being treated the same as the other boys in the building project and construction of the boat. He continued being resentful and angry even when it was pointed out that they were only following the doctor's orders. It was as if he could not accept the fact that they were all trying to help him, after his fall from the truck. These episodes of his not being reasonable and unpleasantly argumentative were becoming more frequent. The majority of the time, he was like the old Matt. He would seem to be totally normal, just like in the old days, and then something would happen, or someone would say something he did not agree with, and suddenly his personality would change. He became accusatory and defensive. It was as if he suddenly believed that he was being made fun of; that the others were picking on him. The strangest part of these personality changes, it seemed to Greg, was that it never happened when Skipper was around. Also, if he was behaving strangely, and saying something totally unreasonable, he would stop, and revert to his normal self, the moment Skipper walked up or joined the conversation.

On one occasion, when the three of them were working on the boat, he got so worked up, mad and agitated that he suddenly turned on Greg, and with his face red and contorted in to a fierce grimace, he shouted,

"One of these days, I'm gonna beat the shit out you Greg. I think you're a fucking asshole, the way you act and behave like a know it all. You're always so prim and proper when Skipper is around, and then you treat me like a piece of crap when no one is looking." he said.

Greg had no time to respond or even think about what Matt had said, because at that moment, Skipper walked up to them. He had been working in the shed.

"What's going on? Did somebody mention my name?" he asked.

In the blink of an eye, Matt reverted, and turned back to his other self, then he said,

"We were just having a little talk Skipper. Nothing important, it's time we got back to work." Later that day, Greg asked Tommy,

"What did you think happened with Matt today? I don't remember saying anything negative to him, and I certainly did not do anything to him"

"I don't know what to think. I know he's different from the old days. It's like he has this really short fuse, and he seems to get upset so easily." Tommy said.

"Yeah, that's for sure, but he's never threatened me before, and I don't remember doing anything, or saying anything to him today to set him off." said Greg.

"I know, It's strange. It's like what ever it is, brews inside of him, and then it erupts suddenly. It doesn't seem to make any sense about what sets him off. It is as if he hears things or imagines things, inside of his own head." said Tommy.

"You're right, it's like a geyser or a volcano in side him. It goes off without any logical explanation. It seems like he thinks or imagines we are against him or trying to hurt him." said Greg.

"Do you think there is anything we can do to help him?" asked Tommy.

"I wish there was something we could think of or know what to do for him. Skipper says to give him more time. That's what we have to do. That's all we can do for now" said Greg.

CHAPTER 37

BOBBY JOINS THE GROUP

One Saturday morning as they were finishing breakfast, Skipper asked the group,

"With summer coming up in a few months, I was thinking we could use another boy here at the ranch. Somebody to fill in for Joe. What do you boys all think of our latest scout member? His name is Bobby Thornton. He seems like the kind of guy who could fit right in. And, I think we could use another pair of hands"

"I agree with you, Skipper. We are used to having four persons. He seems like a really good guy. I haven't spent much time with him yet, but that is easily remedied." said Matt.

"So far, all you're choices have been right on Skipper. You always seem to find the right kind of boys, so what ever you think, works for me." Mrs. Parker said.

"That goes for me too." said Lindsey.

"From what I have seen of him, I think he will fit right in with our group." said Greg.

With in a month all arrangements were completed. They visited with Bobby's parents. The boys told them what life was like, being a scout, living and working at the ranch. They emphasized how great an experience it was for a boy to live at a place like the ranch where he was able to camp out, go fishing and participate in projects like working on the boat they were building. The parents were impressed enough to give their permission that night, and arrangements were made to pick Bobby up on the next Friday evening.

Greg was pleased to have another boy join the group. He liked Bobby from the moment he got in the car. He liked to laugh a lot, and he had a tendency to laugh at his own jokes before he had finished telling the joke. They all discovered that when Bobby was around they would never be bored. He had a story for every situation, and any new story would remind him of another joke. Greg had never spent much time with any body like Bobby. He wondered how a person could remember so many stories and jokes. They started the moment he was out of bed in the morning, and didn't stop until he was back in bed in the evening and falling asleep. He tended to be a little overweight, and that made it even more of a surprise when they discovered that he was one of the fastest members on the track team. His specialty was the quarter mile, but he was also on the relay teams for all sprints under the quarter mile. He had dark brown hair that he wore in a crew cut. He was three inches taller than Greg, and weighed fifteen pounds more. This made him the biggest and the strongest of the four boys. He had brown eyes that seemed to twinkle as he laughed and told his jokes. He had an unnerving way of seeming to know what you were going to say, before you said it.

He loved it at the ranch from the moment he arrived and saw it, but when he saw the boat house, and the railroad tracks mounted on the timbers from the ranch, he could hardly contain his excitement. He said that he could already visualize how wonderful their life would be when the boat was there, and up on the rails. He liked the water and liked to swim as much as Greg. The two of them immediately began to make plans to explore in more detail the large under water grotto in front of the house.

"I can't wait to get in there and check out those big gar you guys saw. We have to figure out a way to catch one." It didn't take Greg long to discover that Bobby had as much, if not more, energy than any one he had ever known. He was also more fun to be with, since he had a never ending supply of jokes with which to entertain, and he was pleasant to be around.

It was interesting to Tommy and Greg, they noted, that since Bobby started coming to the ranch, there was a significant change for the better in Matt. He did not seem to go off unexpectedly into his episodes of strange behavior, as much. Tommy and Greg talked about the change and the difference they observed. They both agreed about the significant improvement for the better in his personality. They had no ready explanation for this change in his behavior. They both agreed about one thing, it was definitely for the better, and they appreciated the change whatever the reason was. Why had the arrival of Bobby brought about such a dramatic improvement, or was it something else they could not understand. Was it something unrelated to Bobby? Since neither of them had discussed in detail Matt's unusual behavioral changes with Skipper, they elected to keep their observations to themselves. As long as he was getting back to his old and normal self, all was well, they thought.

CHAPTER 38

FISHING WITH BOBBY

THERE WAS NOW LESS than two months of school before summer vacation. They discussed among themselves the timing of moving the boat over to the water. Because there would be no one around to keep an eye on the boat until the boys could be there more of the time; the decision was made to move it after school was out. That way someone would be there to see how well the boat sat on the rails over an extended period of time. They would be able to see if there was some asymmetrical settling of the timbers, and be able to take corrective measures if necessary. Delaying the moving of the boat would give them an opportunity to stock the boat house with the necessary provisions for the summer. Until then they could also get Bobby acquainted with the ranch. They would also have more time to plan the summer's activities.

They wanted Bobby to spend some time camping with the Parkers. He had never camped out and gone trot line fishing at night. He did not know what a trot line was. He had never heard of one. They wanted him to experience it all. Sleeping by the fire, and waking up to run the trot line several times during the night. They purposely did not tell Bobby about all the alligators they would see late at night when they rowed the boat out on the lake to remove their catches from the trot line. They wanted to see the surprised look on his face when they turned the flash lights on. They knew from experience how startling it was to see so many pairs of eyes light up all over the lake. They also wanted Bobby to experience how wonderful it was to be cooking and eating the fresh fish, brought out of the lake only moments before, and cooked over an open fire. They knew how delicious the fish tasted, when it was cooked the way Mrs. Parker liked to cook it.

As an appetizer, they would put salt and pepper on some the freshly cleaned fish and rub it in well; run a skewer through it's middle, and cook it slowly over the coals. Then eat it directly off the skewer. They shared this appetizer while Mrs. Parker took some of the fish, coated them with egg white, flour and cornmeal, then she cooked them in butter, in the iron skillet over the edge of the fire. They also cooked potatoes and ears of corn in the coals. While sitting around the fire, watching the fish cook, they listened to the sounds of the night. They liked the sounds the frogs and crickets made. They would hear bull frogs croaking, and alligators grunting and talking to each other. Being so close to the water, they could hear the waves gently lapping at the shore line, whenever the wind picked up. They ate their fish and drank Mrs. Parkers camp coffee. All of these special experiences were what they wanted to share with Bobby.

Mrs. Parker and Lindsey liked these outings with the boys. They enjoyed the outdoor life, and they enjoyed sharing their knowledge and skills with them. They were devoted to Skipper because of his beneficial influence on Mrs. Parker's son. He had been going in the wrong direction for the past year or so. The police were already watching him, and had talked to Mrs. Parker twice. Mrs. Parker liked to tell how Skipper had helped her son get out of trouble with the law, and turn his life around. She thought it was a good message for the boys. In those days both she and her husband worked long hours, and were not around after school, when he needed them most. Now he was in the Army; in officers candidate school. They were very proud of his recovery, and gave Skipper most of the credit.

Living and working at the ranch was a wonderful opportunity for them. They appreciated what Skipper had done for them and their son. They enjoyed helping Skipper make these and others boys lives more enjoyable. They felt more like an aunt and uncle to the boys than caretakers. For the Parkers it was more like being in an extended family. They were happy to have the opportunity to share these special nights with the boys, even though they were getting older. The boys did most of the heavy work, and the Parkers gave orders and instructions. They were in on the boys plan of not telling Bobby what to expect until they were out on the water. They also enjoyed seeing the way new comers reacted to suddenly becoming aware of being surrounded by so many alligators.

They all loaded up in the Ford truck in the late afternoon, and arrived at the lake just before darkness descended upon the lake. They hauled the boat down to the water from high up on the bank where they had left it the last trip. They collected enough wood for the nights fire. While it was still light enough, they baited the series of hooks attached to the trot line they had strung across the usual stretch of water. For the next hour, they sat around the fire; talking and drinking coffee. When they ran the trot line the first time, they returned with a large lake trout and two large mouth bass, and three catfish, enough to start feeding every one. Two hours later and after cleaning and eating their portion of salt and pepper fish, Lindsey said,

"O.K. boys, let's go see what we've caught so far. I'll go the first time with just three of you. Tommy, you have done this the most, and have the most experience. You stay on shore with Mrs. Parker. You'll go out the next time with the other boys."

They rowed the boat out in the lake to where the trot line began. Lindsey said,

"O.K. Bobby, you man the flash light, the rest of us will take the fish off the hooks." There was no moon light, and without the flashlight, the darkness of the night was complete. The quietness on the lake was frequently broken by short raspy grunts of what sounded like large bull frogs, some far away, others much closer. Bobby switched on the flash light.

"Shine the light over here so we can pick up the end of our line." said Lindsey.

After they picked up the line, Lindsey said,

"Let's take a look around the lake. Go ahead Bobby, shine that light around." When the light scanned the surface of the lake, Bobby suddenly exclaimed.

"My God, it looks like dozens of pairs of burning cigars, all over the lake. What the devil is causing that?" All of the boys were smiling silently in the boat.,

"We were all waiting for your reaction, when you first saw all those lighted cigars on the lake. Those are all alligators. That's their eyes shining back at us." said Lindsey. Bobby kept shining the light around, finally he said, "Jeepers, there's so many of them. I'd be scared to death if I were out here by myself." Matt who had been unusually quiet until now, said,

"We thought you would be surprised, and I bet you would have never guessed there could be so many alligators in one lake. We were all waiting for your reaction." said Matt.

"You're right about that, I never would have guessed there could be that many alligators. It must be safe to be out here, right?" he asked nervously.

"We've never had any trouble yet. I think they are all fed so well, they have no interest in us?" Greg said.

When they were back at the fire, Lindsey said,

"You boys go out, next time. Have fun, but be careful. You have your pliers in case you get some catfish, and you have your knives, right?"

"We're all set." said Tommy.

When they arrived at the trot line, they could see the line moving side ways and then being dragged under the water. They knew there had to be something big out there on the line. The first few snoods, the short vertical lines attached to the main line, had catfish on the hooks. They retrieved them using the pliers; then smacked the heads against the boat's side to keep them from thrashing around on the bottom of the boat. They quickly broke off the spines, so as not to get impaled accidentally. The next few snoods were empty; the bait gone. After rebating the empty hooks with chicken guts, they moved on down the line. They could see the main line becoming more agitated. Tommy was walking the line with his hands, pulling the boat along. He reported to the others that it felt like something heavy pulling irregularly against him. With the flash light shining the way ahead, they all could see the water swirling and churning about twenty feet away.

"Greg you better get up here beside me, this guy feels pretty big, whatever it is. It may take both of us to get it in the boat." Tommy said.

"You don't think it could be an alligator, do you?" asked Bobby.

"Nah! It's never happened before. Alligators like something bigger to eat than our little baits." said Tommy, and then added, "Just in case, You grab that oar Matt, and you get that iron pipe there beside you Bobby." As they got closer to the snood, the churning in the water became more agitated. By shining the light directly down into the water, they could tell it was not a big alligator, if it was an alligator, it was a small one. They still could not make out what it was on the line. What ever it was, it was darkly colored, and did not reflect enough light, to make the diagnosis.

"All right everybody, are you ready?" asked Tommy in a loud, excited voice.

"Greg, You and I will pull at the same time. I think, with both of us pulling, we can get it in the boat. You guys get ready back there, in case you need to whack it. Are you ready, Greg?"

"Yeah, I'm ready." said Greg. "O.K. then. Let's do this."

They grabbed on to the main trot line, one on each side of the snood. They bent over, and pulled upward simultaneously with all their strength. When the creature broke clear of the waters hold, the resistance diminished. Their combined strength caused the creature to fly up out of the water, over the gunwale, and into the bottom of the boat. It landed at their feet. Tommy and Greg almost fell backwards into the water with the sudden release of weight. The stunned boys were now looking down at a very large, loudly hissing, grunting, and very angry snapping turtle. It was huge, and occupied half of the bottom of the boat. It immediately started scuttling around on the bottom of the boat; looking for an escape.

"Keep out of it's way!" yelled Tommy. The two boys in the back of the boat clambered up on the rear seat; Matt clinging on to Bobby. Bobby almost lost control of the flash light. Tommy and Greg, who were now sitting on the bow of the boat, quickly put their feet up and over the sides. The angry turtle was crawling around the bottom of the boat with the hook and line still in its mouth. The hissing, grunting sounds issuing from its throat were magnified in the close confines of the boat, and the stillness of the night. The scraping sounds of the claws, and the snapping of the jaws were very unnerving. The snood was becoming entangled in its legs.

"O.K. wise guys. You caught it now let's see you eat it?" said Bobby.

"Stop moving around you two." said Greg.

"We don't want to turn the boat over. Give me a minute to think. What ever you do, don't let him get a hold of you with those jaws. They say even if you cut it's head off, it won't let go until the next sundown."

They all looked at one another expectantly. Suddenly Greg started laughing, and before long, they all joined in, chuckling at the spot they were in.

"O.K., I think I got It." said Greg.

"Got what?" said Tommy.

"The solution, for this thing." said Greg.

"O.K., let's hear it." said Bobby from the back of the boat, as he kept his eyes on the angry, hissing turtle, who was scuttling rapidly around the bottom of the boat, first going one way and then the other; continuing to make those loud awful sounds.

"This will work, as long as the hook holds." said Greg.

"And if it doesn't?" asked Tommy.

"We will cross that bridge when we get to it." said Greg.

"Let's hear your plan." said Matt.

O.K., We put it back in, just like we got it out of the water. Come on Tommy, grab on to one side of the trot line, and let's lift it back in. Then we cut the snood, and we are finished with the darn thing."

"Are you sure you don't want to keep it, and make a pet of it?" Bobby said, with a chuckle. "Or, we could eat him." he added.

"Not me, I don't like this snapping turtle." said Matt. "So please! Just get it overboard." he added nervously.

They both lifted up on the trot line, pulling the turtle up on to the gunwale. Bobby used the oar to help lift up the rear end of the turtle.

"Bobby, you use the oar, and push his butt over when get him balanced on the edge." said Greg.

The turtle made a loud splash when it tumbled over and hit the water. When they cut the snood free from the main line, the turtle disappeared, back down in to the darkness of the lake, the cut snood trailing after it.

Back at camp, sitting by the fire, they all had a good laugh.

"I would have given a dollar to have seen you boys faces when that turtle landed in the boat." said Lindsey. "I know one thing." said Bobby. "Fishing with you guys is highly entertaining, better than a school play anytime, but I don't want to be in a small boat with you guys and a snapping turtle crawling around free, again."

"You boys are lucky it wasn't a big Alligator Turtle. They can get up to a hundred and fifty pounds in weight, and be five feet in diameter." said Lindsey.

"I don't think one that big would fit in our boat." said Tommy.

"You guys leave me out of catching any more turtles." said Bobby.

"Me too!" said Matt.

CHAPTER 39

SCOUT

WHEN SCHOOL WAS OVER for the year, they found more time was needed to have the boat ready to move it over to Hudson. It took them another three weeks to have it completed. The excitement was universal among all the participants. Skipper was there for the first weekend. Skipper's brother hauled the boat to Hudson with his big truck. They bought enough provisions for an extended stay. They were all pleased at how easily the boat was able to be moved in and out of the water on the rails. They were all now eager to take the boat out in the Gulf of Mexico. Plans were made for the maiden voyage the next morning. During dinner that night Skipper made an announcement.

"Well boys, as you know, this day has been a long time coming. From the time we first made the decision to build our boat and berth her here on the water, it has been more than a year. With your help and persistent determination we are finally here. I think we should drink a toast to our accomplishment." Every one raised their glass of root-beer, and took a long drink of the ice cold, sweet, and uniquely tasting beverage. Then Skipper said,

"We need to come up with a name for our boat, and of course every boat needs a captain. I have made the decision of who our captain will be. It was a difficult choice, naturally, as you would expect. Each and every one of you could do the job. I know that, you know that, and I believe it. But, as you all know only one person can be the captain. That person also has to assume the responsibility for every one else on board, and make the decisions for the boats safety. After thinking about this for a long time, I am going to appoint Greg the captain."

Greg quickly glanced around. He could see the feeling of disappointment in Matt's face. Matt looked down for a second, and then a smile broke out on his face, as he looked up at Skipper and said,

"I agree with you Skipper, Greg is the right person. He has been studying hard on how to handle a boat since we first decided to build the boat."

"Here! Here!" said Tommy and Bobby simultaneously.

Both of them looked at Greg. They both had grins of happiness spreading across their faces. Matt also appeared to be happy for Greg.

"This deserves another toast." said Bobby.

After the toast, Skipper said,

"O.K., now that is out of the way, let's get on with choosing a name for the boat."

Matt was the first to speak up,

"What do you guys think of SCOUT, for a name? We are scouts, and it's because we are scouts that we built the boat." he said

"I agree with Matt, it is a perfect name, it matches us and the boat." said Tommy.

"I can't think of any thing better. What do you think Captain Greg?" asked Bobby.

"The final decision is really up to Skipper, I think. It is his boat. He is the reason we are all here, and the reason the boat is here. I think Matt got it right though the first time around. We are all scouts, and the boat will be used to scout out the waters all around here. Skipper should have the final word however, so what do you think Skipper?"

"I cannot think of any thing better, nor more appropriate than Scout, so Scout it is, and Scout it shall be. You boys can paint the name on the stern whenever you have the time." Skipper said.

Greg could see that Matt was extremely pleased when every one agreed with his choice for the boats name. Greg was pleased at how smoothly this portion of the evening went. He expected someone in the group to not be exactly thrilled when he was appointed the captain of SCOUT. Now that it was over, he was looking forward to tomorrow morning. They would be taking SCOUT out for the first time. He would be at the wheel. He would be in charge and giving the orders. He had been studying the charts for some time now, and felt as if he knew the channels in and around their inlet like the back of his hand. It was going to be exciting seeing things for real, and not just on paper. They had already put the fishing gear on board. After breakfast they would launch the boat down the ramp, and head out to sea for the first time.

PART 4

CHAPTER 40

FISHING WITH SKIPPER

When morning finally came, and with the first hint of visible light, Greg was awake with excitement and anticipation. When Skipper awoke, Greg announced,

"Skipper, this is your day to relax and enjoy. We're going to make you breakfast, and then take you out into the Gulf for a day of fishing. Tonight we're going to make you a delicious dinner from the fish we catch today. If we don't catch anything, then it will be hotdogs with pork and beans, our favorite meal when we are here by ourselves. We want you to know how much we appreciate you and all the things we get to do, because of you."

"Well, all right then boys. I will do my best to relax and enjoy the day. If it is pork and beans with hotdogs, that is fine with me too. I will be very surprised if we do not catch something. We just need to learn where the fish like to hang out. That will come with time. Speaking of fish; I want to swim with you tomorrow morning and check out those big fish you think are gar. I will be very surprised if they really are true alligator gar. I was reading about them, and this is not their typical habitat. It would be unusual for them to be this far south in the gulf. They do like brackish water, which is something we do have here, but they usually do not like to hang out as deep as you described." said Skipper.

"O.K. Skipper, sounds great, we have a mask and snorkel that will fit you." said Tommy.

With all four boys working, they had a breakfast of bacon and eggs, with hot cakes ready within half an hour. They made coffee the usual way for themselves; coffee grounds into the boiling water and poured through a strainer. They liked they could make it as strong as they all wanted, and then add milk as required for color. Honey was their sweetener of choice. When breakfast was over, Greg said,

"I'll do the dishes tonight before dinner. Lets all get ready and go fishing now."

They floated the boat, and tied it off the sea wall, in front of the house. When everyone was aboard, Greg took the wheel, started the engine, made sure it was running smoothly, and gave his first order as captain, "Stand by to cast off. Bobby, you go forward. Check that anchor and make sure the anchor line is not fowled in case we need it quickly for an emergency."

All's clear on the anchor and anchor line, captain." said Bobby.

"Cast off bow and stern dock lines. Push her bow away from the wall with that oar." said Greg. When they were floating free, Greg put the transmission in forward, gave it a little fuel with the lever, and they were under way, smoothly departing the seawall. The boat glided quietly over the still, deep water of their underwater grotto. Greg did a three sixty degree turn, going around the expanse of clear, deep, smooth water in front of the house.

"Every one look over the sides. See if you can spot any of those big fish anywhere." said Greg.

As they cruised over near the other side, and just before Greg turned the boat back towards the house, Tommy yelled,

"Here they are! I can see them, right below me. I can see four of them. They seem to be going in and out of a type of cave or a ledge, or something like that."

"That's good, now we know where to start looking tomorrow morning." said Skipper.

Greg completed his 360 degree turn, then stayed in the middle of the channel as he steered the boat around the first three markers at the bends in the channel. Just as he cleared the last channel marker, and before the open water stretched to a visual infinity, Bobby, who was forward and standing on the cabin top, cried out,

"Oh my God. Look quick, over to starboard, there is a huge ray passing under us. He's just cruising along slowly, he'll be going past the stern any second now." They all got to see it, as it passed slowly under them. It was a deep gray color. The wing span was at least ten feet, maybe more. It moved its wings ever so slightly as it cruised under them, and out of sight.

"Boys, this is what it's going to be all about. Now that we can get out here in the deeper waters of the Gulf, we will be able to see things we would never have the opportunity to see ashore. With our boat we are cruising into a strange new wilderness. We have no conception yet of the amount of life that exists beneath us. Now we will have an opportunity to do some discovering on our own. I can just imagine how Daniel Boon must have felt every time he saw a new territory, and the animals in it. That ray was such a beautiful and magnificent animal. I have never seen one in the wild before, and I've never seen one that big." said Skipper.

He no sooner had gotten the words out of his mouth, when the ray erupted from the water behind them, it leapt clear of the water, some forty yards off the stern. As it hit the water on reentrance, they could hear the huge splash. It sounded as if someone had thrown a horse in to the water. The water splashed ten to fifteen feet high into the sky, creating a series of rainbow colors and light bands that quickly vanished. They assumed the beautiful spectacle was caused by the effects of the splashed droplets of water reflecting the sun light, which was coming from behind their stern. Then they were in the Gulf of Mexico with the spectacle they had just witnessed only yards away, and moments behind them. It was a matter of history now, not witnessed, it would have never happened, as far as any one would ever know.

The color of the water under the boat was a light green. The sun was on a slant off the water, coming from behind the boat. It was one of those beautiful days in central Florida that made the whole crew happy to be there. It was a gorgeous, sun drenched day. The sun was already starting to get hot, so they all took off their shirts and splashed water on themselves and each other. Then they stripped down and got into their bathing suits They cruised due west for half an hour, stopping periodically to determine the depth of the water with the lead line. The water depth stayed at around fifteen to twenty feet, and it appeared to be an all sand bottom, judging by the material that stuck to the wax on the tip of the lead. Soon they saw where the water changed color to a darker blue, further west, out in the distance. Greg steered the boat in that direction. He had no intention of getting out of sight of land. He wanted to be able to see the markers by which he could identify their inlet. When they were half way to the darker water they were joined by a pod of dolphin. They counted eight of them as they swam in front of the boat, and to the sides, surfing on the bow wave. They swam in and out of the wave created by the bow. They swam on both sides of the boat. Swimming sometimes only partially under water and then occasionally leaping completely out of the water. They were constantly disappearing and then reappearing, over and over again. Every one enjoyed watching them frolicking around the boat, and then just as suddenly they were gone. Greg felt a sense of disappointment and sadness as he became aware that the dolphins were not coming back again. He wanted them to stay with the boat and continue making their first boating experience in SCOUT even more enjoyable.

As they approached the darker water, Greg said,

"Get ready with that lead line." As they passed over the color change in the water, Greg said," Let's see how deep it is here, drop that line in now Bobby." After a few minutes passed Bobby said,

"Oh yeah, it's over sixty feet here. That means we passed directly over a ledge of some type. It's twenty feet and then drops off to more than sixty feet suddenly."

"What's your plan Greg?" Skipper asked.

"I think we should drop our anchor in the shallow water, drift back and fish this deeper water. This is the first deepwater we have seen. We might as well check it out, and see what's down there." said Greg excitedly.

"Bobby, you drop the anchor when I call for it. I am going to come about, and position the bow over the bank. Then we can drift back over the deeper water, and we can fish the ledge."

After they backed down on the anchor and securely set it, they increased the scope by letting out on the anchor line and positioned the boat over the sheer almost vertical ledge. Within ten minutes they all had a line in the water. Every one was using shrimp as bait at first. They all started catching fish right away. Sheeps heads, Snapper, Sea Bass. After an hour of fishing, Skipper said,

"You definitely picked the right spot today captain. We already have enough fish for several meals, so I'm going to try something different, just for fun."

He chose one of the live medium sized Snapper they had just caught, and using a larger hook, ran the hook through the upper, lower back so it could swim freely. He dropped it over board and let the heavy sinker carry the fish down near the bottom. He then pulled it up a few feet, and then sat down to wait and to watch his crew. Skipper enjoyed watching the boys having so much fun. It gave him great pleasure to be able to provide opportunities for his boys to be able to learn about boating and fishing like this. He only wished he could offer more boys these types of experiences. It was a beautiful day, with just enough breeze to keep them comfortable. The high clouds were large and fluffy, and periodically blocked the sun, creating temporary shade for a few minutes. The boys were now catching so many fish, they started choosing which ones they wanted to keep for eating. The rejects they did not want to keep they carefully removed the hooks from them, and returned them to the water. Greg noticed that Matt fished standing next to Bobby as much as possible. If Bobby changed his location, it wasn't long before Matt changed his also. When lunch time came and Bobby chose a seat to eat his sandwich, Matt chose a place to sit close to Bobby. Matt seemed to offer to get things or do things for Bobby more than Greg had ever noticed before. Bobby joked with Matt a lot it seemed, but then it was hard not to; Bobby was always joking, and Matt was always right next to him. Tommy was talking with Skipper. He had already caught as many fish as he wanted for the moment, and he was now taking a break. He had just opened a soft drink for himself and Skipper, and was in the process of sitting back down, when Skipper's rod jerked violently downward. Skipper only had one hand loosely on the rod as he reached for his drink. He had been sitting there for half an hour with no bites. He was not ready for what happened next. The rod was almost dislodged from his hand by the sudden force. He had to drop his drink in order to maintain control of the rod and not lose it overboard. Skipper quickly loosened the drag on the reel, and then they all watched as the line began to run off the reel. The fish was moving away from the boat, going south, paralleling the vertical bank. Skipper began to tighten down on the drag, but as he did so, the rod bent over almost double, and he quickly loosened the drag again. Greg was watching the line going out of the reel, trying to determine how much line was left on the reel. He made the decision instantly for what he did next. He grabbed a life vest as he passed through the cabin. When he arrived at the bow and stem of the boat, where the anchor line was secured, he quickly untied the bowline knot. He retied another bowline knot to the vest and tossed it and the anchor line overboard through the forward hatch. When he returned to the aft part of the boat, he could see that Skipper was still struggling to find the right amount of reel drag so as not to break the line or the rod.

"O.K. Skipper, were free of the anchor now. I'm going to start the engine so we can go with him. You'll have to keep your line away from the propeller, we can now follow this beast to New Port Richie, if we have to." Greg said.

With the engine running, Greg could change from neutral to forward and then reverse or what ever was necessary to follow and fight the fish, or what ever it was on the line. Skipper was working hard. He was struggling to keep the rod from breaking. He moved around to the stern of the boat. He managed to keep the reel drag at the right resistance to minimize the strain on the line and the rod. Greg did his best to keep the boat following the fish, backing the boat to ward the pulling line. So far Skipper had not been able to gain any line back on the reel.

"Bobby, come over here and take this rod from me. I'm getting a cramp in my hand and can't stay with him much longer" Skipper said.

"I don't want to be the one to lose him." said Bobby.

"Don't worry about that, this is a team effort. If you don't help now, we'll lose it anyway." said Skipper.

"Tommy and Matt, you guys take some compass sightings on the shore. Line something up so we can come back and find our anchor when this is all over." said Greg.

"I really want to see what this thing is." he added.

"Hey guys, give me some pointers here. I don't know any thing about fighting monsters of the deep. I'm not proud. I'll take any advice." said Bobby.

Just then the rod bent over, and the drag started clicking rapidly, signaling another attempt at a run and escape.

"Ease up on that drag some." said Skipper," it's this knob, here." He said, pointing with his index finger.

"Just keep him away from the prop. Let me know if he starts coming back at you." said Greg.

"All right, we've both taken some sightings; now what can we do to help?" said Matt.

"Stand by to help Bobby. You might have to take over the rod. Get a bucket of water ready to pour over him if he gets too hot. He' already sweating heavily." said Greg.

The line kept moving steadily away toward the South. Bobby had started to gain some of the line back on the reel. He was covered with perspiration now with the constant effort of pulling up and back on the rod, and then reeling as fast as he could, only to lose it again in the next slow run it made. Matt was standing next to Bobby, splashing him with water, and giving him swallows of iced drinking water to try to cool him down. Skipper was sitting with his back against the back of the cabin; watching things happen. He had a smile on his face. He was very pleased at how the day was evolving. His boys were having fun, they had already caught all the fish they could eat. What ever happens now is for fun, sport and entertainment, he thought.

After another thirty minutes passed Bobby said,

"It's somebody else's turn to fight this thing. My arms are killing me. Matt, you take a turn for a while."

Matt took the rod, and began trying to reel in the line. He had the same experience as Bobby and Skipper, every time he gained some line, he lost it again. Then it stopped going south and turned back in the direction from which they had come. Greg circled the boat, keeping Matt in the stern. After another twenty minutes he said, "I think it's time for someone else to take over. My arms are falling off." Matt said.

"I'll try it." said Tommy. He took charge of the rod. After fighting for almost an hour, he said, "I'm done in, this is ridiculous. We haven't gained on it any."

"Let me try again, I'm rested now." said Bobby. He had the same experience as before. Nothing any of them did made any difference in the effort to bring the fish closer to the surface.

"I don't think we can catch this thing. Maybe if we fought on for a few days, but not today, and not now. We need to return home before dark. What do you think Skipper?" said Greg.

"I think you're right about us not catching it now. I do think every one should have a say on this, because we have all been involved with it. Of course, if you as the captain feel we need to go in now for safety reasons, that's the end of the discussion." said Skipper.

"We could stay out another hour, if everyone wants. Who votes for another hour of this?" asked Greg.

"I don't think we can catch this thing, on this tackle given another month. I'm ready to vote to quit now." said Tommy.

"I don't think we can catch this thing, or what ever it is, unless we get a submarine to chase it. And then hit it with a torpedo." said Bobby.

"I agree. We would never bring this fish in unless it dies of a heart attack or old age." said Matt.

"That settles the issue. I'll cut the line, just to say I had something to do with it." said Greg.

After he cut the line, Greg turned the boat and set a course to line up the objects on shore that Tommy and Matt had taken a sighting on when they buoyed the anchor with the life vest. In half an hour they sighted the life vest bobbing in the water. They retrieved the anchor and set a course for their inlet, and home.

In another two hours they had the boat out of the water, up on the boat carriage, and had started cleaning the fish. They cooked half of the days fish catch, and refrigerated the rest. They also cooked some grits, made a cabbage salad, and sat down to eat.

"There's nothing like fresh fish cooked in butter, and some grits with cheese melted in for extra flavor." said Tommy, as he took a sip of his iced tea, and started loading his fork with another piece of the buttery fish.

"What do you guys think we had on the line today?" asked Tommy.

"Every body gets three guesses. We don't know what it was, and probably will never know, but it will be fun to guess. Who wants to go first?" asked Greg.

"Let's look at the facts, and what we think we know." said Skipper. "It was alive because it moved around. It was big enough to take the whole fish we used as bait. It obviously had to be very big, because we didn't have any effect on it with our biggest tackle. Also, It didn't change depths once we got it on the line. That should narrow the parameters some." he added.

"I think it was a big fish." said Matt. "Like a big grouper." he added.

"It could have been a shark, but I don't think so. I've heard they like to fight if you hook them." said Tommy.

"Yeah, This fish acted like we were not even there. Just went where ever it wanted. It could have been a giant turtle. Yeah, that's it, because we're good at catching turtles." said Bobby with a broad grin.

"I'll stop by the library or better yet, buy us a book that helps identify fish in the Gulf and bring it with me next week. Then we will be better able to look up and know what we catch, and perhaps not catch, like today." said Skipper.

"Great idea Skipper. Now that we can go out in the Gulf whenever we want, there are an infinite number of different kinds of fish we could catch, it will be fun to be able to look them up and learn what they are." said Greg.

"My guess for now, is it's some kind of giant Grouper, or Jewfish, I've heard they can get really big; some times as much as several hundred pounds" said Tommy.

"We will probably never know what it was we had on the line today, but we can certainly get better informed." said Skipper.

CHAPTER 41

SWIMMING WITH SKIPPER

THE NEXT MORNING THEY were up early. Greg and Bobby volunteered to make breakfast for every one. Bacon, eggs, pancakes with honey, and camp coffee. When breakfast was over, and they were on their last cup of coffee, Bobby said,

"Skipper, you said you wanted to swim with us this morning, to look at those big fish. We're ready whenever you are."

"We're going, but we need to wait an hour, we need to get this big breakfast out of our stomachs. We don't want any one getting cramps." said Skipper.

"Do you want to dive from the boat or swim from the shore?" asked Greg.

"I want to take the boat. That way we don't have to swim so far." said Matt.

"That's fine with me. The more experience we have with launching and retrieving the boat the better. It will get easier and easier." said Greg.

"I'll anchor over the shallow bank on our side of the deep water, and maybe, if we're lucky we can dive down right on top of them, if they're where they were yesterday. The tides going out, so we should drift back over that area. We only have four masks, so we will have to rotate who the look out is."

"We should put the dock lines out. That way we have something to hang on to, so we can rest in the water between dives." said Bobby.

"No problem, we have plenty of them" said Greg.

After they anchored and drifted back, Greg said, "I'm going to dive on the anchor, and make sure it's dug in, we don't the boat to go any where unexpectedly. When he surfaced from checking the anchor, he said, "We're secure, this boat is not going any where. Who wants to be the first look out?" asked Greg.

"I want to swim with Skipper and Bobby." said Matt.

"O.K., I'll be the look out." said Greg.

"No. You're already in the water Greg. I'll take the first look out." said Tommy.

Greg knew Matt was not as strong a swimmer as Bobby and himself, it made sense for Matt to be in the water and swim with Skipper. When the swimmers were all in the water, and hanging on to the attached dock lines, they could effortlessly look down and all around.

Skipper could now see, for the first time, why the boys were so excited and had been so impressed with their new front yard. It was like being in a huge under water aquarium, except for the fact that it had been created by nature, instead of man. It was fifty to seventy feet deep in places. He could barely see across to the side walls, and around the periphery of this natural aquarium, even though the water was impressively clean and clear. It was like being in a huge under water grotto with the steepness of the walls and the unusual depth. There were multiple deep horizontal recesses carved into the vertical walls as they rose up from the bottom. Most of the recesses were down much deeper, and they could have easily been caves, or even tunnels, possibly connecting to other grottos, or some shallow estuaries at some distant sites, he thought. Without diving down deep, to the cavernous openings, to look horizontally into them it was impossible to know for sure. Skipper noted that the water in which they swam was brackish to the taste, it definitely lacked the intensity of the Gulf's salinity. A clear indication of the amount of fresh water coming from the spring. As Skipper looked down and around, he too, was impressed with the size and beauty of this natural aquarium, in front of his house. The clarity of the water added to his appreciation for the spectacular beauty of this unique natural phenomenon. The underwater dimensions were roughly the size a foot ball field. At the limits of visibility towards the opposite side of the grotto, there appeared to be several more of the stalagmite type wall structures coming up from the bottom. Some were ten, fifteen and twenty feet high. There were several schools of smaller fish around them, but the majority of the larger schools tended to be on the opposite side, in the direction of the outlet toward the Gulf of Mexico.

"I don't see those large fish yet. Let's swim over and see what's on the other side of that big wall like structure coming up from the bottom." said Skipper. As they all made progress swimming in the intended direction, Greg could see that Matt swam with an awkward, totally inefficient type of dog paddle stroke. All the other swimmers used variations of a breast stroke, or side stroke as they swam and leisurely looked around. Greg slowed and circled back around and got behind Matt, he wanted his observations to be undetected by Matt. By the time they arrived on the other side of the wall like structure, they were forty yards away from the boat. Every one but Matt was comfortable and relaxed, maintaining smooth, evenly paced strokes. Greg stayed either behind Matt, or off to the side, out of Matt's field of vision. Greg began to get the impression that Matt was struggling much more than he should have been, after such a short swim. Just then Bobby yelled out, "Hey everybody! Over here, they're over here." Bobby was about twenty yards away from Matt and Greg. Every one began to converge on Bobby, who was treading water and pointing down; every now and then he raised his arms in the air and spread his arms wide apart, trying to indicate how big the fish were that he was seeing. Every one but Matt was now looking down at the bottom. Greg left Matt, as it was such a short distance to the fish, and cruised easily over to the tallest of the wall like structures, he saw three long, cylindrical shapes. They were dark olive and brown in color. They were about ten to fifteen feet off the bottom, and ten feet apart. When Greg got directly over them he could see that the snouts were very long, more than twice as long as the rest of the head. They had dark spots along the sides. The fish were five to six feet long, and appeared to be lying motionless. He could see the fins moving smoothly and rhythmically. Matt was still ten yards away, but moving slowly towards him.

"Come on over here Matt. I've got a great view of them. What do you think Skipper? Can you see them from there?" asked Bobby.

"Oh yes. I can see them. They are not the monsters I thought I was going to see. They are long, but probably do not weigh more than forty or fifty pounds."

Every one but Matt was hanging semi vertical in the water, face down, or treading water, resting as they watched. Matt was still trying to make his way over to them. Bobby now became aware of Matt's struggling, eased his way over, and got closer to Matt. Now he could see how tired Matt was becoming. Matt was now fighting the water, awkwardly, just trying to keep moving, and to keep his head above water; The expression on his face indicated the fear he was feeling. He would soon be nearing the point of exhaustion, followed by fear and then panic, Bobby thought as he remembered his lifeguard training instructors words.

"Hey Matt, try to hang in the water, like we're doing. Try to rest and save your energy." said Bobby.

Matt tried to copy the others, but when he stopped moving his arms and legs, he sank down, with his face beneath the water; it was now obvious to Bobby, he could not rest, and he could not swim. He was expending twice as much energy, just trying to keep his head above water. When Skipper became aware of the situation, he swam smoothly and calmly with strong strokes up next to Matt.

"How is it going? Are you doing all right?" He asked.

"No! I'm tired! I'm really tired!" Matt gasped.

"O.K., O.K., No problem." said Skipper. "I am going to turn around. I want you to grab on to my neck and shoulders and just rest. Don't try to swim. Just hang on, I'm going to take us both back to the boat. Bobby you stay with me. Greg you get back to the boat. Get the heaving line and some life vests ready."

Greg swam as fast as he could. When he got to the boat, he started climbing the rope ladder, into the boat. As he was climbing he was yelling to Tommy, to get the life vests from the cabin. Once on deck he grabbed the heaving line, and attached a life vest to the weighted heaving end. Now, he took the time to watch the trios progress.

Matt did his best to hang on to Skippers neck, but his hands and arms were too tired and failed him; as his grasp released, he immediately sank downward, almost vertically. As he sank, he involuntarily sucked in air to cry out, but it was water, not air, that entered his mouth and nose and flooded his lower pharynx. When the water splashed his vocal cords, they went into immediate and complete spasm; he could no longer get air in or water out of his lungs. The horrific panic of not being able to breathe was instantaneous. He began thrashing out at the water in all directions. Bobby who was facing him could see the over whelming, terminal, fear in his eyes. His panicked thrashing made it difficult to approach him from any direction except from behind.

"I'll take him in Skipper. I know how. I've done it before. Stay close by, just in case." Bobby said.

He quickly maneuvered around and got behind Matt, who was now sinking further down. His panicked thrashing subsided as he began to lose consciousness, and then he stopped moving completely. Bobby then dove and reached down. He grabbed Matt by the hair with his left hand, and pulled him up to the surface. He got his face out of the water, then he passed his right arm around Matt's neck and across his upper chest, grabbing him under his left axilla. This maneuver held Matt's face clear of the water. Bobby started swimming toward the boat, pulling strongly with his left arm and cupped hand. He was resting Matt's upper back on his right hip. The laryngeal spasm had still not released, but Matt had stopped struggling; he remained an unconscious passenger all the way to the vest Greg had thrown them. Skipper was apprehensive but calm, as he swam along beside the pair. As Bobby approached the vest he grabbed on to the life line and the vest Greg had heaved his way.

"Give me another vest." he called out. With the two vests he was buoyed enough to support himself and keep Matt's face out of the water. He could now rest some himself.

"We will never be able to get him into the boat as long as he is unconscious. Can you hang on until I can get you to shore?" said Greg.

"Yes! No problem. I've got him." said Bobby. Just then the laryngeal spasm broke and Matt emitted a small hooping sound, then a gasping coughing spell ensued, followed by more hooping and whistling type sounds. He immediately began struggling again, flailing away at the water, trying to break free from Bobby's hold. He was not yet aware of what was happening to him. His frantic, flailing movements slowly decreased as more air began to move in and out of his lungs, and some oxygen rich blood began to perfuse his brain again. Skipper now said, "I'm going to stand on the ladder. I can hold him from here and keep his head above the water until we're back ashore. As soon as I'm secure, pass him to me. Stay clear of the prop Bobby, until the engine is off."

By the time they reached the shore, and could stand on the bottom, Matt was awake enough to be aware of the circumstances. He let himself be towed through the water, and stopped resisting his rescue. He was still coughing. It was now apparent the amount of water he had aspirated was minimal.

Several minutes passed, Matt was slowly getting back to breathing normally. Fortunately only a minimal amount of water had entered his trachea before the laryngeal spasm happened. The only remnant of the near disaster was the stark, terrifying memory now filed away in each of the rescuers brains.

CHAPTER 42

REVELATIONS

LATER THAT NIGHT, AFTER they prepared and ate another fish dinner, with fried onions and potatoes and a mixed salad, they talked over the days events. They discussed what they had seen while in the water.

"I'm going to reserve my judgment about what kind of fish they are until we get our book next week end." said Skipper. "I'm almost sure they're not Alligator Gar, because they're supposed to be larger than the ones we saw today. The nose on the fish we saw today is long, and they had rows of spots. They could be a Spotted Gar, but I think they're smaller than the ones we saw today. Anybody have any other ideas, or think something else?" asked Skipper. Greg waited a minute. He wanted to see if any one else offered information. When no one spoke, he said,

"I spent a little time in the library after we saw them the first time. I read some stuff in the encyclopedia."

"What did you find out?" asked Tommy.

"What I remember is, there are three different kinds of Gar. There is an Alligator Gar, a Spotted and a Long Nose Gar. The Alligator is the biggest. They can be ten feet long, and weigh as much four hundred pounds. The Long-Nose Gar has a long nose. They can be six feet long and weigh fifty pounds. The Spotted Gar's the smallest. They're three feet and weigh eight to ten pounds, and have spots on the sides. What I read said it would be unusual for

Alligator Gar to be this far south in Florida, but I guess any thing's possible. The length of the snouts on these makes them either the Long Nose type or some kind of mixed cross breed."

"So, you just happened to be in the library, and just happened to run across articles on gar?" asked Bobby, with eyes open wider than normal, and a hint of a smile forming on his lips.

"No. I didn't just happen to be there. After we saw them, I wanted to know more about them."

"Oh, I know that. I'm just joking you." said Bobby, with a grin and a wink.

"Don't you know yet, Greg's our resident book worm. The only thing missing is the horned rimmed glasses?" said Tommy, smiling at Greg.

"Hey guys, take it easy on me. I just happen to have too much time on my hands when I'm at home." said Greg. "Besides that, Skipper's always telling us how important it is to try to read more. Isn't that right Skipper?"

"Of course it is, and I'm proud of all you boys for taking me seriously about that kind of stuff." said Skipper.

"What else do you remember from what you read Greg?" asked Bobby.

"Not much more. It did say most gar do like brackish water, and we certainly have that because of the fresh water spring. Another thing it said, they like to be near the surface of quiet water, that doesn't fit here, they were definitely deep. A couple of other things I remember, the roe of the Long Nose Gar is poisonous when eaten by man, and there are some unsubstantiated reports of Alligator Gar attacking man."

"Well, I think that gives us enough information to say they are probably Long Nose Gar or some type of cross breed. Maybe we'll know more after we get our new fish and reptile book for the house; I can see right now, we'll be using it a lot in the future." said Skipper.

"I didn't get to go today, so I can't wait to see them for my self." said Tommy

Tommy's statement caused Matt to suddenly develop an unhappy expression on his face. Then he said,

"Hey guys, I'm sorry I ruined your day. I didn't mean to almost drown you know. I didn't do it on purpose. I didn't try to ruin your day Tommy"

"Of course you didn't do it on purpose Matt, no body blames you. It was just an accident." said Skipper

"And, Like any other accident, we should look for ways to make sure we do not repeat it. So we should discuss what happened, and why and learn how not to let it happen again. Don't you agree Matt?" asked Skipper.

"Yes, but it was me that ruined the day for everybody, not one of you. It makes me feel really bad inside and I don't like to feel bad." Matt said.

"Of course not, no one likes to feel bad. But if there is something to be learned, anything that can benefit any one else we should look for those answers. We should all always try to learn from our mistakes, and then once we learn, we move on with life, and try not to do it again. We don't want to make the same mistake twice. So let's take a look at today to see what happened. We need to see if there is anything that can prevent it from happening again." said Skipper.

"So Matt, let's begin with, what do you remember about today?" he asked.

"O.K. Skipper, this is what I remember. I was swimming along with you all. I thought I was doing all right, and then I started feeling tired. It seemed like the more tired I became, the more afraid I was. I remember getting so tired I couldn't swim anymore. Then, you were there Skipper, I remember holding on to you, but my arms got too tired to even hang on to you. And, when I couldn't hang on any more, something bad happened. I couldn't breathe any more. I blacked out. The next thing I remember was being dragged through the water, and you holding me Skipper. Then everything started to be O.K., and I could breathe again. Is that what happened?" he asked.

"Yes. But, you should know, it was Bobby who saved you, and kept you from going to the bottom. It was he who he brought you back to the boat after you blacked out and were sinking down. You owe him a big one this time." Skipper said with his friendliest smile.

"What caused you to become unconscious was water splashing on your vocal cords." said Skipper.

"So, how did water touching my vocal cords make me become unconscious?" asked Matt with a puzzled expression on his face.

"It goes something like this; if any type of liquid touches the vocal cords, they can go into spasm. When they are in spasm, no air can get into the lungs, and no air can get out the lungs. It's a reflex, I think it is supposed to keep you from drowning in the short term. As long as the vocal cords are in spasm, no more air can go in or out of the lungs, and no more liquid can go down your trachea, or wind pipe. I think yours must have stayed in spasm until you passed out from lack of oxygenated blood getting to your brain." said Skipper.

"What happened after I passed out?" asked Matt.

"Bobby took over and rescued you. By the time he handed you over to me, you were waking up."

"Thank you Bobby. How did you know to do that?" asked Matt, looking fondly and admiringly at Bobby.

"I just did what they taught me in the lifeguard water safety course. I took it last summer. You have to know what to do, and be strong enough to do it. Fortunately, it worked out, just like the book says it's supposed to." said Bobby.

"The real question is why did you get so tired so fast? The way I see it is if you had not got so tired, the rest would not have happened." he added.

"I'm not as good a swimmer as all of you. I don't think I was honest with myself about it until today. I began to realize it when I saw how easily you swam away from me. I think that is what started making me afraid. I also remember seeing Greg coming back to check on me. I didn't want him to see me struggling."

When he said this, Tommy and Greg glanced over at each other. They suddenly shared a mutual comprehension. They remembered how Matt had unexpectedly turned on Greg that afternoon they were building the boat. It was obvious now, Matt did not like Greg anymore.

"Why would you say that Matt? Maybe if you had said something to him, none of this would have happened." said Skipper.

"I don't know really. Maybe it's because I feel like we are in some kind of competition. I didn't want him to know I was struggling. Be sides, if he cared so much about me, he should have said something, or done something right then, instead of letting me almost drown. He doesn't care at all about me." Matt said, developing a scornful frown as he looked at Greg.

"Oh Matt, that's not true. Of course I care about you. I was coming back to check on you. I wanted to help you if you needed it." Greg said.

"You can't fool me Greg. I know you don't like me. I can feel it. You have never liked me, not from the very beginning. Another thing I just thought about, you should have never let me sit up on the cab of the truck that day. I think that was mostly your fault too, just like today. If it were not for you being here, none of those bad things would have happened to me." Matt exclaimed.

After Matt finished this last statement, there were some very confused looks around the group. Except for Matt, who was glaring at Greg with extreme dislike, if not outright hatred, showing on his face.

"Well Matt, we had no idea you felt that way about Greg. I think you must be having some kind of a negative reaction to nearly drowning. I think you'll feel differently again when the frightful emotion of a near death experience passes." said Skipper.

It took a few seconds, then Matt's face gradually appeared to change again. The obvious look of hatred began to disappear from his face. A slight smile began to form at the corners of his mouth. As the seconds passed, it appeared to all of them that his face progressively changed into a more benign appearance. It was as if he suddenly realized, and became aware that his passionate display of dislike for Greg was a mistake. His facial expressions slowly but progressively continued to change. They could see the way he felt in how his face looked. Slowly at first, and then more rapidly, he began to change how he looked right before their eyes. As his facial expression changed he reverted, and started looking like the friend he was during their recent dinner."

"Oh, of course, that's it, Skipper's right. It was a bad reaction to nearly drowning. I'm sorry about that guys. I'm ashamed of myself for behaving like that and saying that kind of stuff. That was some silly stuff I said. I don't know what came over me. I can see that now. I certainly didn't mean it. I want to take it all back. Will you all please forgive me. Please!" said Matt, looking around imploringly.

"Of course we forgive you Matt. We understand how an awful experience like that can affect you and make you say things you don't really mean." said Skipper.

"I forgive you Matt. I can only imagine how I would feel after going through an experience like that." said Greg, as he walked over and gave Matt a hug.

"I would never do any thing to hurt you; just like you would never do anything to hurt me." he added.

"Hey, no problem here, buddy. I can understand it." said Bobby.

"I'm sure I would have freaked out myself. No bad feelings on my part." said Tommy.

"Thanks guys; I'm so sorry. I will never understand how I could say something so silly like that. It will never happen again, believe me. It will never happen again, because I don't really feel that way." he said as he looked around and smiled at everyone. By now he was looking like Matt had looked before, calm, serene and peaceful.

CHAPTER 43

SKIPPER'S NEW RULES

THE NEXT MORNING THEY were all having breakfast with Skipper before he left for work.

"You know boys, I've been thinking about some things. After yesterday's accident, I don't want Matt to go swimming without a life vest. I want him to wear one that we are sure will keep him above water, no matter how tired he is. I know we have some on board that we bought for every one else in an emergency, but when I come back next weekend I will bring one that I know for sure will always be reliable and do the job. We cannot take a risk with Matt's life until he gets much better at swimming on his own. As long as you promise to follow these new rules of mine until I return, I am comfortable letting you stay here by your selves, and I'm comfortable with your going out in the boat."

"What ever you say Skipper. What ever kinds of rules you want us to follow is good with us. Right guys?" said Greg.

Each of the boys agreed. What ever Skipper wanted them to do would be fine.

"All right then, here is what I insist on. Every one has to wear a vest when you go swimming. I do not want Matt swimming at all, until I get back with his special vest. I will try to be back here Friday or Saturday at the latest. When you go out fishing in the boat, every one has to wear their vest at all times. I want Matt secured with a jackline attached to him and his life vest, any time he is on the boat. Another thing, unless I am on the boat with you, I don't want any one of you swimming in the Gulf from the boat. Is that perfectly clear? Does every one understand me? Are there any questions?" asked Skipper.

After every one personally agreed, Skipper added, "As I said before, Greg is the captain of the boat. His word is the law, no exceptions. You have plenty of food, and we will go shopping again next week end. Make a list if there is any thing special you need or want. Have a fun week."

With that said, he was gone and the boys were on their own for the next five to six days.

"O.K., what do you guys want to do first, I mean after we get the dishes done? asked Greg.

"First thing for me is to see those big fish you guys saw yesterday. Then we should do some more fishing from the boat, out in the Gulf." said Tommy.

"Sounds good to me. We better get the things we need for the jackline first." said Bobby.

"What is a jack line?" asked Matt.

"I'll let the captain explain it, since I'm not completely sure my self." said Bobby.

"A jackline is a system of ropes or straps that are meant to keep a person onboard the boat, or to be more precise, to keep the person attached to the boat. Everybody who comes up on deck wears one when the weather is bad. We tie one end of a stout line to the bow, and the other end to the stern of the boat. Then we connect a shorter line from Matt to the longer line which is attached to the boat. We create a loop where we attach the shorterline to the longer line. It allows that person to move around, forward and aft, so they can work on the boat, but still be securely attached. Even if that person goes overboard for any reason, they are still attached to the boat. Since they are connected to the boat by the system of lines, they are already found, and you don't have to worry about finding them. Sailors who go out solo, usually wear them, because if they go overboard by accident, there's no one to get them back in the boat. It's perfect for anyone who is not a really a good swimmer. From now on, we will all work together to help Matt become a better swimmer." said Greg.

"It sounds like a good idea to me. It's always better to be safe than sorry." said Matt, smiling as he looked at Bobby.

"Since we're going to take the boat out fishing, we might as well use it to see the gar first; just like yesterday." said Greg.

They anchored the boat close to where the fish were the previous day. They put out the rope ladder for boarding the boat. Greg dove down on the anchor to make sure it was securely hooked. Matt and his life vest were attached to the jackline, just as Skipper required. The other boys all put on their life vests. Before going into the water Greg asked,

"Are you comfortable being the look out Matt? We are going to be close to the boat, so you can hail us if other boats approach, or if anything unexpected should arise."

"Yes. I can handle that. I'll have a coke while you guys look at the fish." Matt said, already turning toward the cooler. They entered the water with their goggles on, and after looking around to find the underwater structures, began swimming away from the boat, spreading out from each other as they moved away. It was Bobby who saw them first. They were in a different location from the day before. When Bobby called out that he had sighted them, Tommy and Greg started swimming over to him. Then Tommy looked up and yelled,

"Hey guys, there's two more of them over here."

"That's great, let's swim around and see how many of them we can find." said Bobby.

Several times they got together to compare their sightings, then swam off again in different directions only to get together again in a different location. This went on for about an hour. When they climbed back on board they were excited to share with Matt what they had seen. They found Matt in a somewhat truculent frame of mind. He was not interested in hearing about what they had seen. As they talked excitedly about the different types of fish, and the number of Gar they had seen. Matt interrupted them suddenly, with,

"Why don't we just go on and get under way. I'm bored and hot with having to sit here, all by myself, the whole morning."

Tommy looked at Greg with a quizzical expression, as if to acknowledge what was on his mind about Matt's very first comment on their return. Greg simply said,

"All right then, let's get that anchor up, and head out to sea. Bobby would you please go forward and bring in the anchor after I steer the boat over it and break it free. We want to get Matt out where he can have some fun too."

This brought a slight smile of acknowledgement from Matt, before he turned a blank stare west, out toward the vast and receding emptiness of open water.

CHAPTER 44

GULF FISHING

GREG STEERED THE BOAT out toward the location where they had previously hooked on to the unknown sea creature. They triangulated their location by compass shore sightings and then dropped the anchor. Fishing was good. In two hours they had caught as much as they could eat for a couple of days. They stopped fishing to eat lunch. Bobby said,

"While we are eating, I want to see what kind of response we get if I throw in some of our cut up bait. I'll string it on a fishing line with some floaters so it doesn't sink. It might be entertaining to see what shows up." Matt, as usual, whenever Bobby made a suggestion, was the first to reply,

"That's a great idea Bobby. I'll help you prepare it." he said.

"I think it will be fun too Bobby, we just need to make sure we don't get any lines wrapped around our propeller. I don't think a small fishing line would cause us a big problem, but something like a dock line wrapped around the prop would require someone to dive under the boat to clear the prop, or we could be stuck out here." Greg said.

"We know there are a lot of fish feeding here right now, because we've already caught so many; so there must be some big ones down there feeding on them." Bobby said.

Bobby and Matt strung twenty or so large chunks of cut up fish on a piece of mono filament fishing line. They added a few corks to make sure the bait ring stayed on the surface. They tied the two ends together, making a circular ring of the chunks of bait. They then attached another long line to the circular bait ring with the pieces of fish. They slipped it over board on the starboard side forward, near the bow.

"I don't want this any where near the prop." Bobby said.

After ten minutes, some smaller fish began to show up and make quick, darting movements in toward the bait ring, tearing small chunks off the fleshier pieces. Bobby was standing on the roof of the cabin top, looking down into the water. He was holding the end of the line attached to the bait ring. He said he could see some larger dark shadows and an occasional brief flash of a lighter color coming up from down deep. The shadows seemed to disappear as if passing under the boat and then suddenly reappear again. He could not be sure, so he said,

"You guys should get up here with me, so you can see better. I think we just might see some action and have some sport before too long."

All the boys climbed up on the cabin top, and stood near Bobby, looking down into the water; first focusing on the ring of bait, and then trying to change their focus to see deeper down in to the water. Soon, some larger Sheepshead and then some Snapper began to appear, and approach the bait ring. After a few moments they began to feed on the larger chunks of bait. They pulled the ring of bait first one way and then another. The pieces of fish were too large for them to eat the whole thing, so they tore smaller pieces off the larger chunks one bite at a time. As they watched, the ring of bait was slowly shrinking in size. Suddenly, they saw a flash of bright movement come from under the boat. The streak of movement was like lightening, it was so fast. At first, they could not make out what it was, but once it hit one of the larger Snapper, it slowed enough for them to identify it as a two foot long Barracuda, with large jagged, razor sharp teeth exposed, as it struck. Most of the Snapper disappeared with the barracuda, as it swam back under the boat, leaving a stream of blood. Just as quickly as it disappeared, two more slightly smaller Barracuda struck other feeding fish. The ring of bait was becoming hard to see because of the cloud of blood mixed with chunks of fish floating free on the surface. Just as quickly as it started, it ended. There were no more fish to be seen, only the cloud of blood surrounding the bait ring, and it was slowly spreading out, sinking down and dissipating. The boys all looked at one another in a knowing way, like 'That was a great idea.' Thinking that the fun was over Tommy and Greg started to climb down from the cabin top, when they heard Bobby say,

"Oh my God! Look at this would you! That has to be the largest Hammerhead Shark I have ever seen." As the boys all stared down in the water they could see the unmistakable signature shape of the shark's head as it slowly cruised in to approach the cloud of blood. It looked to be about ten feet long and two and a half feet in diameter. The shape of the laterally expanded head, with an eye on each end of the stalk, made the head take on the shape of a double headed hammer. The huge fish slowly cruised passed the boat, the eyes at the ends of the stalks seemed to be looking at the boys on the cabin top. As they all watched intensely, it cruised away for about forty feet, then it made a slow turn, and began heading back toward them, and made one more pass through the disappearing blood cloud. Determining there was nothing of greater significance to eat, it turned on it's side and opened it's jaws, clamped down on a thicker portion of the bait ring and swam off in the direction it had come. When the fishing line came taut, Bobby threw the end he was holding into the water, and watched it trailing after the now disappearing shark.

"Well that was certainly worth while, don't you think?" said Bobby.

"Yeah. You do have a good idea every now and then." Greg said with his familiar grin. All the boys were now smiling at each other, then Tommy said,

"I think that little experience deserves a refreshing cold drink."

That night, as they were eating their fish dinner, with grits and coleslaw, Greg said,

"I've been thinking, maybe we shouldn't tell Skipper about this shark adventure. He might consider it a little too risky for us to be chumming up giant man-eaters. What do you guys think?"

"I agree with you on that one Greg. I certainly do not think we should tell him about my latest idea, and my next plan either." said Bobby.

CHAPTER 45

FISHING FOR SHARK

"OH, OH. WHAT ARE you thinking now, Bobby?" asked Matt.

"Watching that shark swim off with our fishing line in his mouth, made me think, what if we had a big hook and a big line attached to our bow. Then what? Maybe, just maybe, we could catch ourselves a really big fish. That would be fun. Don't you think?" He said with excitement in his voice.

"I think it sounds like a great idea Bobby." said Matt.

"It sounds dangerous to me." said Tommy.

"Me too." said Greg.

"Well, look at it this way. If it gets too risky, we simply cast off or cut the line attached to our boat. Then the shark goes on his merry way and we go on our merry way. If we catch him, we could maybe make some extra money selling it. There is a commercial fish house a mile or so up the coast. I bet we could sell it there." Bobby said

The boys talked excitedly about Bobby's plan, for the next half hour.

"I think we should take a vote and see how many of us want to participate in this adventure. Of course, Greg has the final say so, we all know that. He is the captain and has the last word, Skipper made that very clear." Bobby said.

"How many of you guys really want to do this shark thing?" asked Greg.

"I do!" All three responded simultaneously.

"O.K., O.K. guys. I get the picture. Let me think about it over night. I mean, after all, I am the one who is responsible for the boat, and all of you." said Greg.

After the dinner dishes were done, and a round of cards played, Greg said,

"I've been thinking about it, and I am going to vote with the rest of you on this great shark hunt. If you can be ready, we'll go in the morning. The weather is going to be perfect, just like today."

When the excitement of Greg's announcement subsided, Bobby said,

"First thing in the morning, I'll ride the bike into the tackle store. I saw some gigantic hooks just the size we want, the last time I was in there. We will also need some steel wire leader, and about fifty feet of really stout line. That should do the job."

"While you are in the store, the rest of us will make some sandwiches, and load the boat with ice, drinks and some bait for catching our chum." said Greg.

That night Greg slept fitfully. He had a dream about his boat being rammed by an angry giant shark. The boat started taking on water, and they were all bailing as fast and as hard as they could. They were losing the battle and the boat was beginning to sink. That was when Greg awoke, startled, and sat straight up in bed. It was pitch black dark in the cabin, and every one else appeared to be sleeping soundly.

"I sure hope that is not a portent of things to come." Greg said to himself, before drifting slowly off, back to sleep.

CHAPTER 46

SHARK FISHING!!!

By the time Bobby returned from the bait and tackle store, the boat was loaded and ready to cast off the lines. There was a strong feeling of excitement palpable on the boat, shared by all the boys. They all watched intently as Bobby showed them the hooks he had found at the store. One was ten inches long from the tip of the barb to the hub where he used a pair of pliers to twist on a six foot piece of thick wire leader.

"I'll do the rest when we're under way." Bobby said to the watching onlookers.

"So what do you think Greg? Do you want to try the same place for starters?" Bobby asked.

"That's been my plan from the beginning. There is something special and uniquely different about that location; with huge unknown monster fish, and a beautiful Hammerhead shark. That is the only place to go to on this day." Greg said.

"Every time we go there something interesting happens. I sure wish we could get a look at the terrain on the bottom there. I think there is something different and special going on down there. Maybe some sort of an explosion of some kind. I have heard that they used the open waters west of the keys for a bombing range practice in World War Two. As a result there are now many large holes, and some deep caves that have been formed as a result of the bombings. The fishing is supposed to be very good there."

I'll bet that one day we will have some sort of technology that can read what is going on at the bottom of the oceans." Greg said.

Matt already had his life vest on and was attached to the jackline. He was helping Bobby, who with avid attention and interest was working on the hook, leader and line to be used on their shark fishing expedition. A shark or something as big as a shark was what they hoped to catch. Tommy was cutting and preparing the bait to be used for attracting the bigger fish. Greg was steering the boat down the last leg of the channel. The open waters of the Gulf were dead ahead. The sun seemed uncommonly bright for so early in the day. The breeze was negligible, so the water was flat, and that made it nearly impossible for any one looking in the right direction to miss the large spotted ray as it cleared the water only four feet from the side of the boat Matt was sitting on. Only Matt and Greg were looking in that direction; the now air born Leopard Ray, was flying fast when it smacked head first in to the side of the boat, just below the gunwale. The loud thump of the collision, and the jolt of the impact, caused the boys to look, and Greg to cut all engine speed. This action brought all the others to the side of the boat. When they looked over the side, they could see the ray slowly sinking downward, toward the bottom. It was obviously stunned or even more seriously injured. Now, it was resting on the bottom, in fifteen feet of water, it appeared to be about three to four feet in diameter. It was not making any effort to swim, just lying motionless on the bottom. As the tide was coming in there was a tidal current flowing in to shore, and the ray moved gently with the current. Greg yelled to Bobby,

"Throw the anchor forward, right now!" Bobby quickly followed orders and in moments the boat came to a stop. The ray was lying motionless on the bottom, now near the bow of the boat. Bobby was looking straight down on the ray.

"We can get that ray in the boat if you want Captain Greg. It's not that deep where it's at. I can dive down and attach a line to it." he said.

"I think it would be easy to do too Bobby, but I don't think any of us can do it with a life vest on. That was one of Skippers rules, remember, and we all agreed to follow the rules. It's too bad we don't have a harpoon or something like that." said Greg.

"Yes, like a spear gun, then maybe even with our vest on we could get it." said Tommy, and then he added, "It sure is beautiful, look at those spots. It looks like a really healthy leopard's skin with all those spots."

As they stood looking down at the ray on the bottom, talking over their options of retrieving the ray with the gear they had on board, and before any one had a good idea, the ray began to move it's wings in an undulating motion, slowly at first, and then gradually began moving them a little faster. They watched as it slowly moved off toward deeper water. It then went on out of sight.

"Well, that problem took care of it self. We don't have to think about it any more now." said Greg.

"It sure was beautiful, I've never seen one like that before, with all those beautiful spots." said Tommy.

"O.K. let's get that anchor up and head on out to our own spot." said Greg.

After they triangulated their location with shore sightings, and were securely anchored, they started catching fish on a regular basis. When they had enough fish for dinner, and enough to make a satisfactory bait ring, Bobby finished cutting up the larger fish. He left the smaller ones in tact except for making an incision on the ventral surface. He wanted to let the intestines hang out. After they had enough to make the bait ring, they still had the bait bucket half full of fish, fish parts and intestines, all floating in thick blood and seawater.

"Hey Matt, take the bait bucket and put it in the corner at the back of the boat and cover it with something to protect it from the sun." Bobby said.

"Sure thing Bobby." Matt said with a sniff, as he looked at him with his unique smile reserved for special persons.

He saved the biggest snapper, keeping it intact, to place their big hook in it. He started it in the mouth and brought the hook out the ventral surface, near the anal opening. He anchored the shank of the hook and the wire leader at the mouth with a separate piece of strong wire. This left a significant circle of the very sharp barbed hook exposed. The exposed hook looked menacing and dangerous. He then attached it to the bait ring using a separate piece of wire.

"The more blood the better." he said.

"Then we better hope for another Barracuda or two. They sure make a bloody mess when they eat." said Matt.

"You would too, if you had teeth like them." said Bobby, with a friendly pat on the shoulder.

"If everyone is ready we can put in some chum and blood with the bait ring; then we will see what kind of excitement the deep brings us." said Bobby.

"Ready when you are." said Greg.

Bobby and Matt, working together, slid the bait in to the water at the front of the boat. Tommy and Greg cast out some of the chum pieces, and they poured some of the bloody water over the side. Then, they all sat down on the cabin top to watch and wait.

It was only about ten to fifteen minutes before some smaller feeding fish began to gather around the bait ring; the chumming having attracted them first. They were now working on the smaller pieces of fish. It was entertaining to watch the different levels and sizes of fish feeding. There was now half a dozen or more of one and two pound fish feeding on the bait ring when the first Barracuda streaked in and hit one of them. It was an impressive sight. The fish was cut in two, the larger piece disappearing under the boat with the Barracuda. The back half was still wiggling as it started to descend. It was almost out of sight, when Bobby who was now standing and looking down at the disappearing segment, exclaimed,

"Oh, Oh, get ready something big just grabbed that other half of fish. When it opened its mouth, I could see something white and wide before it took the piece away."

"Greg was looking out over the open water when he saw two, and then three fins, thirty or forty yards off, slicing smoothly through the water, coming in their direction. They were sharks, and had obviously picked up on the dissipating blood trail, and were now coming in to find the source.

"Here they come, we got sharks!"Greg announced excitedly.

The largest of the gray shapes reached the ring first. It was about eight feet long. The other two were only slightly shorter. Their backs were gray, and when they rolled for a turn, they could see the whiteness of the bellies. The snouts were surprisingly long and pointed. The tips of the fins were dark black. When the first shark opened its mouth to claim several large pieces of fish from the ring, the boys could see the sharply pointed erect front teeth. When the shark swung around to escape with its capture of the pieces, the line making the bait ring, parted, and separated. The shark bite had obviously cut the bait ring line in two. The two larger end pieces floated free. As the shark swung around to make off, it's tail got impaled on the sharp point of the tip of the large hook which was exposed from the belly of the intact bait fish. Bobby was not prepared for this eventuality, he had not yet secured the bitter end of the heavier fishing line to the boat. Immediately the line began paying off too quickly, as the shark swam away. Greg was in the cockpit of the boat. Bobby was still on the cabin top. He started looking for the end of the fishing line.

"Grab that line and pass it to me so I can secure it to something." Greg yelled.

Bobby immediately fell to his knees on top of the line. He grabbed the line, which was now moving out too quickly with the shark, and tried to slow it down. Tommy was also now on his knees, he immediately started scrambling to find the end. When he finally identified it in the coils, he grabbed it and passed it into the cockpit to Greg. Bobby was able to slow the struggling fish only a small amount, but it was enough time for Greg to take several turns to the midship cleat. Greg yelled out,

"We got it secure down here, don't hurt your hands any more. Can you eventually secure the line you are holding to the bow in anyway. By lying on his stomach and crawling and inching forward, sometimes on his knees, he was able to take the line with him, little by little he managed to get a half hitch around the stem post, and then another. The boat immediately swung around sharply, lined up, and followed behind the shark, which was now frantically trying to escape the pursuing boat. Greg seeing what was going to happen next, took off his vest and passed it to Bobby.

"Take this and tie it to the anchor line and throw it overboard. Whatever you do don't stand up, we got sharks all over the place down here. Get back down here with us as soon as you can, crawl if you have to." Greg ordered

The boat now started following the shark in a more or less straight line. Everyone took a deep breath, and looked at each other.

"What now?" asked Tommy.

"Let's just catch our breath for a moment. Every body relax," said Greg.

"O.K. I got it. We'll let him pull us for a while and let him get tired. With the four of us we should be able to pull the shark close enough to the boat where we can gaff it. When we get ready to gaff it, we have to free up the line where it is attached to the bow."

"That sounds good to me." said Bobby, "But, let me rest for a while, then I'll go back up there and free the line. I know how I attached it. It won't hurt to let the shark tire himself out a little more."

After Bobby freed the line from the bow stem post, he returned to the cockpit. They cleated it a midship again. The line now streamed from mid ship, and the boat was being pulled sideways. After several more minutes, the shark was showing signs of tiring. The four of them were able to start maneuvering it closer to the boat, a little at a time. When it got close enough, they could all see that the snapper was still securely attached to the hook. The large hook with the snapper was imbedded deeply near the tail of the shark. The snapper, with the hook in it was stuck tightly to the shark's tail, thus creating a ludicrous, almost comical scene. Now they had the shark about ten feet from the boat. They were all very tired from hauling on the line. They took a break to catch their breath. While they were looking down on their catch, the other two sharks began to circle the exhausted shark. It was possible, Greg thought, that the two other sharks could now start to do something ugly, and not expected, right before their eyes. It would be something, that until now, they had only heard about. This could possibly turn into a shark feeding frenzy, a situation where the sharks get so excited, they eat anything in their way, even eat another shark who could not defend itself.

While they watched, the larger of the two circling sharks darted in and struck their shark right behind the gills. Instantly a large chunk of their shark was missing. A startling amount of blood began streaming from the gaping hole. In another instant the second shark swooped in and chopped out another huge chunk.

White strips of flesh protruded and streamed from the gaping wounds. The amount of flowing blood, now obscured their view of the scene, and of exactly what happened next. They could partially see amid the swirling, splashing, churning water that their shark was being torn apart as they watched. The next thing they realized was the line now quickly ran out again. They had carelessly not paid attention to the loose line and the bitter end since they became distracted by the spectacle before them. By all working together, they now managed to secure the line again to the mid ship cleat. Now the boat suddenly healed over, and the rail dipped down toward the water, and the boat started moving sideways again. In another moment, and when the shark moved in to clearer water they all could see why. They were being dragged behind the largest of the sharks. It apparently had swallowed the entire snapper, along with the chunk of shark which had the hook in it. It was now obvious, the shark had swallowed the hook completely and was securely hooked. When they took stock of things, it was apparent they had lost almost all of the hard earned line. They only had a few feet of line attached to the boat before the bitter end. After taking a much needed break to catch their breath, they watched the boat being pulled sideways, with the rail periodically dipping perilously close to the water. After a short while, the speed of the boat slowed significantly. Bobby put on a pair of work gloves and began trying to regain some of the line that had been lost when the shark first made it's run, and caught them off guard. He wrapped a coil over his shoulder, and brought it out by his waist. This gave him better control of the line without hurting his hands as much.

"Tommy, get some gloves on and help me fight this shark. We need to pull it in and gain back some our lost line." said Bobby.

With the two of them now working and hauling on the line, it was easier for them to play the shark. They had it within twenty feet of the boat. The shark suddenly dived under the water, and disappeared from their sight. All they could see was the line, dancing and moving around on the shimmering water's surface, moving first one way, then the other. With all the boys watching, the shark suddenly erupted out of the water's surface. It went straight up and leapt clear of the water. The white belly and dark gray shoulders streaming off wavelets of water as it rose in the air. The black tipped fins were more striking than ever. When it was almost clear of the water, it began spinning rapidly on its long axis, once, then twice. This was only the beginning of a series of spectacular spinning leaps, clear out of the water. Most of the leaps were combined with the rapid spinning maneuvers, which at first startled, and then thrilled the boys as they watched, fascinated. Both Bobby and Tommy were now getting tired of fighting the shark, in spite of the occasional rest they could get when Bobby was able to take a half turn on the midship cleat.

After a period of twenty to thirty minutes, the shark stopped leaping and spinning. It now began to swim toward them. Then it went around and under the boat, repeatedly. The boys did their best to walk around the cockpit, trying to keep the line clear of the propeller, as the shark crisscrossed under the boat. After another twenty minutes the shark suddenly stopped crossing from one side to the other. Then Bobby and Tommy reported, there was no longer the pull of the shark on the line. It was obviously caught and securely fixed on some non yielding structure under the boat. The shark now stayed out of sight, it was obviously under the boat. Every few moments they could feel the boat jerk violently, and they would almost lose their balance. Gradually the jerking motion became less frequent, and less violent. Then gradually, they slowly subsided to an occasional jerk, and for that they were grateful. They could also feel a different kind of muted jolt to the boat periodically. They thought that it must be when the shark bumped up against the bottom of the boat. At those times, they knew it was still under them.

"I'm going to start the engine, and try to put it in gear. We have to know what happens." said Greg.

The engine started and ran smoothly as long as it was in neutral gear. When Greg put it in forward gear, the prop turned over a couple of times. Then it made a dull thunking sound, and killed the engine.

"I think it's time now we all stop and get some rest and refreshments. We also have to face the facts. There is only one thing that line can be attached to on the bottom of our boat, and that thing is our propeller. We may have caught something we come to regret." said Greg.

For the next hour, they peered over the sides, trying to see the shark. Occasionally they saw some parts of it, but it never stayed in view very long. On some of the shark's lunges, the boat jerked violently sideways. They talked about what they could do, and what would have to be done, if somehow the situation did not spontaneously resolve itself. The first option they hoped for was that the shark would free itself. If it did, then someone could dive under the boat, assess the situation, and cut the line free from the propeller shaft. With the shark still hooked, and under the boat, no one really thought it reasonable to go down and check things out. During the first couple of hours they scanned the water in all directions, hoping to see some other boat they could signal for help. It was still always a possibility, but they knew from the past it was rare to spot another boat when they were out fishing.

For the present they were without an anchor, and without use of the engine. They were several miles from shore. It was getting later in the afternoon. There was no one they could signal for help. They were floating free, on the surface of the Gulf of Mexico, at the mercy of the ocean currents, the tides, the weather, and the shark. For the first time, Greg began to feel a sense of desperation. He had not instigated this fiasco, but he had been a willing participant along with his crew. So, as far as he was concerned, he was the one who had allowed this to happen, and he bore the full responsibility. In his mind if any one was going to have to do something risky or even stupidly dangerous, it would have to be him.

"I should have kept the engine running, then maybe I could have maneuvered us away from the darn thing. But, I didn't, and here we are in this bad spot, and I caused it." Greg said.

No one said anything. There wasn't much they could say. They knew there was nothing they could say that would change things for Greg, or how he felt. He was the captain, and he was responsible. He would never feel or believe anything else, and they knew it.

"The answer is fairly simple and straight forward. The line has to removed from the propeller. All I need to do is dive under the boat, and cut the line off. If it were not for the shark being tied under the boat, it would be a simple procedure." said Greg.

"That's true, It would be simple, but there is a shark under the boat, and it is tied to the place where you need to go." said Bobby.

Tommy and Matt nodded their heads knowingly, in agreement with Bobby.

"So, how do we get the shark away from the prop? Let's all try to think of ways to do just that." said Greg.

"O.K. Here is an idea. We tie a knife to our gaff pole. Then we try to stab it when we see it. We make it bleed enough to attract other sharks. They arrive and solve the problem for us." said Tommy.

"That's not a bad idea, except, our gaff pole is too short to reach the shark when we do see it." said Bobby.

"That's true, but maybe we can use a variation of it." said Greg. "The shark is limited to a certain distance from the propeller, because he is tethered to it, so he can't go past the fixed distance of the line's radius from the prop or in other words, what ever the length of line is between the prop and the shark. So, I go in the water with the knife attached to our gaff pole. I stay at a safe distance so that it cannot get to me. Then, I stab it to death, or at least make it bleed enough so that other sharks are attracted, and then I get out of the water before the other sharks arrive to finish off our shark." Greg added.

"It sounds possible, but also very risky and very dangerous." said Bobby.

"Yes, it's risky and it's dangerous, but I think Greg can do it. If anybody can do it Greg can." said Matt.

"Let's keep working on some other possible solutions, for now." said Tommy, looking towards Matt suspiciously.

They talked over several other options for the next half an hour. None of the options were considered a real possibility. Several minutes passed in silence.

"O.K.! Yes! Hey! I think I may have it figured out. I really think this one will work. At least it has a good chance of working, and I am the one who will be in the water with the shark taking the risks." said Greg excitedly.

"All right, let's hear your plan." said Bobby.

"It's simple really. We trap the shark at the bow of the boat. While it's trapped, I go in from the stern and tie a rope to the line going from the prop to the shark. We keep that line secured to the stern. The shark will still be trapped by the same system of ropes, just as it was before. Then, I cut the shark's line free from the prop, but because he is still trapped at the bow, I am still safe. Then all I have to do is remove all the line wrapped around the propeller. Then we turn the shark free, go find our anchor, and we go home and have one of our great dinners." Greg explained, with a smug smile of satisfaction.

"So, just how do we trap the shark at the bow of the boat?" asked Tommy.

"Here is where it gets interesting, and challenging" Greg said. Then he explained. "We tie three of our four dock lines together. Then we put a small weight at the middle of this single new long line. With a person on each side of the boat, each one holding an end of the long line, we walk it forward. From the stern toward the bow, just like they did in the old days, when they keelhauled men. Except we do it in reverse, because they always did it from the bow to the stern when under way. The most important thing we have to do, is get the line to go under the propeller. Once it is forward of the prop, we pull it up snug against the bottom of the boat, and keep walking it forward. As we move that line forward the shark will be pulled along, forced to move forward toward the bow by the dock lines. It will be trapped with its jaws up against the bottom of the bow of the boat. I will use the fourth dock line and secure it to the line attached to the shark from the prop. I then attach that fourth dock line to the stern of the boat. I then cut the line which is attached to the prop and free the shark from the propeller. With the shark being held forward, I can take my time getting the line off of our prop."

"It all sounds so easy now that you have explained it. Except for one thing." said Bobby.

"What's that?" asked Greg.

"Turning that shark loose. We should definitely keep it after all this trouble." Bobby said with a straight face, seconds later he broke out in his familiar grin and jokester's laugh.

"If I don't make it back in the boat, you three can do what ever you want with that darn shark." said Greg.

"Let's get this show on the road, or should I say, in the water. Unless any one has any objections." he added.

"I think it is a brilliant plan, and I am confident Greg can pull it off." said Matt.

Tommy looked at Matt, trying to discern his true feelings.

No one else said a word, so Greg said,

"All right then, here is how we do it. Bobby, you and Tommy will walk the three dock lines, tied together, forward. One of you on the port side, and the other one on the starboard side. When you have him trapped as far forward as possible, you secure your ends of the line to the stem post. I will go down the ladder with my mask and check things out. When I see you have him securely held there, I will tie a line to the rope from the prop to the shark, and secure it to the stern. Then I will be free to take my time cutting the line free from the propeller.

Any questions, any one?" asked Greg.

"What can I do?" Matt asked

"You will be my look out, and you will alert me if you see any other sharks come snooping around while I am under the boat. You will have the most important job." said Greg, and he looked at Matt with a wide smile on his face.

Tommy tied two of the heaviest sinkers to the middle of the rope. They then dropped the rope over the stern, and began walking it forward. When they judged they were forward of the prop, they hauled the rope upward and held it tight against the hull. After moving the rope forward with relative ease for three to four feet, they suddenly felt a strong jolt of resistance, followed by several more rapid and violent jolts.

"Just keep it up tight against the bottom of the boat now, and keep moving forward slowly." said Greg. They both looked up at him and each gave him a big wink. Tommy and Bobby struggled with moving the rope and the shark forward. Eventually they were both as far forward as they could get on the bow, and still be relatively safe and secure themselves. After tying each end of the rope to the bow, at the stem post, they both stood up and looked back at Greg.

"Our part is done, Greg. Let's hope your part goes just as smoothly." said Tommy.

"No one tell Skipper about me not wearing my life vest. I know I promised not to go in the water without wearing it but, we needed it to locate our anchor. I don't think I could have done this with it on anyway."

Greg put his mask on, he looked around at every one and, gave a thumbs up with his right hand. He gave the knife to Matt, saying.

"Be ready to hand it to me. But first go ahead and attach a lanyard to the knife so I can secure it to my wrist while I am in the water. I will call for it as soon as I get this rope tied to the one from the prop to the shark."

With a big smile and a wave to every one, he began descending the stern ladder in to the warm waters of the Gulf. As soon as he put his head under water, he looked forward. What he saw was a very unhappy and agitated shark being held forward at the bow of the boat. Its snout was being held tight, snubbed up against the bottom of the boat. He could see the shiny wire leader coming out of its mouth. Six feet back was the loop in the line, where it was joined to the wire leader. The rope Tommy and Bobby had hauled forward had the wire leader and the shark held forward, trapped up against the bottom of the boat by the joined dock lines.

"So far, all is going according to plan. Where the loop of the line is attached to the wire leader is where I will tie my line." He thought to himself. He surfaced and took several deep breaths. He then went back under water, and swam to the propeller. He then tied his free length of line to the heavy fishing line at the loop for the wire leader. Greg kept glancing towards the shark while he was underwater. He was expecting and always hoping that the shark would be in the same position, at the bow of the boat.

He then surfaced for more fresh air. He took several deep breaths and dove again. He tied a second secure knot to the fishing line. Then he surfaced, and climbed aboard. He tied the free end of this rope to the stern cleat. He then pulled heavily on it several times to convince himself how securely it was attached.

"O.K. Matt, when I am back in the water, hand me the knife. I will be ready to start cutting the shark free from the prop. Then I am going to surface again for more fresh air, and to make sure the shark is still being held forward. If all that looks good, I will go back and keep cutting the line until it is free it from the prop." Greg said.

When he was in the water and ready, he asked,

"How do things look from up there?"

"Right now, all looks good." said Matt.

Greg took the knife in his right hand, attached the lanyard to his wrist, and dived again. When he was at the propeller, he held on to it with his left hand, and started cutting through the heavy fishing line still wrapped tightly several times around the prop. Starting the engine and putting the transmission it gear is what made it so tightly wrapped around the prop. Greg thought. When it was almost released, Greg tested his restraining and safety line, again. It felt secure. He surfaced, looked up at Matt, and said,

"Now all I have to do is free the line wrapped around the prop. It's wrapped around it several times. It make take me a few dives to get it free. Does all still look O.K. from up there? No sharks around?" he asked.

"Yes, all is still good. Does it look like it's going to work?" asked Matt, who was strangely looking at the bottom of the inside of the boat as he spoke.

"Yes, I think so." said Greg.

"I'm going back now to start cutting on the prop ropes." said Greg.

Once he was under the boat again, he checked on the shark, it was still being held in the same place. Greg was sure the shark was looking directly at him. When he got to the propeller, he immediately began sawing with the knife at the wraps of line around the propeller. When he needed air again, he judged he was maybe a third of the way to completion.

"Two or three more times should do it." he said as he broke the surface.

He took in some more deep breaths, and again dove under the boat. When he was ready to start cutting again, he felt a concussive splash at the back of the boat. He turned to look and saw the bait bucket floating on it's side with the blood and fish, and fish pieces spilling out, turning the water a bright red all around the stern of the boat. The water was still clear where he was working, so he kept sawing away with his knife, but he now worked with increased speed and effort. Just before he thought he had to surface again for more fresh air, the last coil of line pulled free from the shaft. Greg surfaced immediately and quickly climbed the ladder. When he was standing on the top of the boarding ladder, he looked at Matt who was standing there, looking at him with a stunned and horrified expression on his face.

"I didn't know what else to do. I thought I could see what looked like a big fish coming up from down deep toward the back of the boat. I knew I needed to warn you quickly in some way. When I looked around, the only thing I could see to throw in the water to scare the fish and warn you was the bait bucket. So I threw it in to alert you, I didn't know what else to do." Matt said defensively.

"Well, I'm back on board the boat now, so no harm was done." said Greg, with a concerned look on his face. He searched Matt's face for any signs of intent.

Bobby now climbed down from the cabin in to the cockpit. Then he could see the water was all red behind the boat.

"What the heck happened? Where did all the blood come from? Did you cut your self?" he asked.

"No, I didn't. I'll let Matt explain how the blood got there." Greg said, and then he quickly added,

"Hey guys, I'm fine, everything's good. We did it. Now, all we have to do is retrieve our dock lines, cut the shark free, and get the heck out of here. I'm ready for an ice cold drink."

It was relatively easy to free the shark from the boat. Bobby released the line attached to the stern. He walked It forward until he reached the wire leader. He had Tommy cut the wire with wire cutters. They removed the restraining rope from the bow. The shark moved very slowly at first, then it gradually began to swim off. The section of wire leader hanging from the shark's mouth produced glints of light in the sun, that sparkled back at them. The shark stayed on the surface, as it swam slowly out of sight. It was apparently going to survive, even though it had been prevented from moving for several minutes. Greg later learned that some sharks that become immobilized for a significant period of time will die. Those sharks apparently need to have water flowing through their gills. It then occurred to him, that if he had known that fact when they had the shark trapped under the boat, he may not have needed to get under the boat with the shark. All he had to do was wait until the shark died from lack of forward motion. But that was then, and he did not know that fact about sharks at the time of crisis.

The boat engine started and ran cleanly, without issue. Greg put the transmission in gear. The boat moved smoothly off like always, as if there had never been the slightest problem. They retrieved their buoyed anchor, and charted a course for home. Bobby and Tommy kept steeling secretive glances at Matt. They did not know, nor could they understand, what was behind his rash decision to throw the bloody water and fish parts into the water with Greg. He must have known that all that blood and fish pieces was certain to draw more sharks to the boat; after all they had been chumming fish and sharks in exactly the same manner.

Neither Tommy nor Bobby thought they would have done that, in spite of Matt's adamant protestations that he had no other options with which to warn Greg.

CHAPTER 47

THE ATTACK

IT WAS TWO DAYS after the shark fishing episode, and the boys were still home bound. The weather had taken a nasty turn for the worse. The night of their return from their shark fishing adventure, a westerly wind brought a storm of heavy rain and wind in from the Gulf. Fierce winds were creating white caps, and spewing foam and water on to and over the sea wall. The change in weather made it impossible to take the boat out in the Gulf.

There had been a gradual diminution in the fury of the storm over the past couple of hours, then there was an unexpected stillness outside. The fierce winds gradually subsided, and the rains no longer pounded the windows. The sun partially returned and illuminated the house and all around the bayou. The boys had just finished a game of cards, in which Greg had been uncommonly lucky. The most unlucky player of all was Matt. It was very obvious from his facial expressions that he was not happy about it.

He stood up and put his hands on the edge of the table.

He leaned on the table and bent over towards Greg. His face became contorted into a mask of hatred and fury.

"You have to be cheating to win that much. Tell us how you are doing it, you cheater. You could not win that much without cheating. You're also a liar. I know—"

Bobby suddenly ended the discussion, when he said.

"Let's go out for a walk, and take advantage of this break in the weather. Maybe we can see those girls who live around the corner."

"Yeah! And, what would we do with them, after we see them?" asked Matt, with a challenging, bellicose look on his face. This was very strange and different behavior, because he was talking to Bobby.

"Maybe introduce ourselves. Maybe become friends. Maybe take them fishing sometime. But if you don't try to aim high, you might hit low and never hit the target." said Bobby, with his usual friendly and comforting smile, that conveyed, "I'm on vacation, don't bother me with trivia".

The boys started their walk along the unpaved dirt road that led out to a point of land overlooking the channel they used to get to the Gulf. The dirt road had been recently worked on with big excavation equipment, and potentially promised items of interest from the dredging and landfill. There were no girls out in the yard. There was no one visible, any where they looked.

When they were half way to the point of land that was their destination, Matt who was walking in front, suddenly turned and cried out loud, to Greg.

"I have had as much as I can handle from you Greg. You told these two friends of mine that I threw those bloody fish parts in to the water to attract a shark; that it was my plan, and that I hoped the sharks would kill and eat you."

The boys all stopped walking. They looked at Matt in amazement. Tommy and Bobby were two persons who knew this accusation was not true. They had never spoken to Greg about the incident, in spite of their own concerns for Matt's use of a well known shark attractant, to warn Greg about a possible shark siting. They didn't have long to consider their concerns. As they watched with stunned expressions on their faces, Matt walked quickly up to Greg. He struck him in the right temple, with a left hook. They could both see the large piece of rock in his left hand. The punch was sharp and clean, it came out of no where, as far as Greg was concerned, he never saw it coming, just as he never considered the possibility of it happening.

Greg felt a heavy blunt impact on the side of his head. There was no pain, just a jarring stunning sensation. It was a numbing, incapacitating force. He was severely stunned, and he felt himself falling. Darkness stalked his consciousness. He fell to the ground, only slightly aware of some diffuse light coming from somewhere. He had no control of his arms or legs. He heard shouting. Someone was yelling at him. When he focused hard on the words, he thought he could hear Matt's voice.

"Get up you bastard. I want to hit you some more, I want to kill you, you son of a bitch." In his darkened confusion, he thought he could see Matt, standing over him with a large rock in his hand.

Greg tried to move, to respond in some way, but he couldn't make it happen, his limbs would not work properly. When Greg did not respond and get up, Matt erupted in to a loud murderous tirade of shouts and curses. He suddenly fell or jumped down on top of Greg; his body pinning Greg beneath him. When he realized Greg could not defend himself, he scrambled around and knelt on him, pinning his arms to the ground with his knees. He immediately started striking Greg with the rock. He was trying to hit Greg in the face and the head as much and as fast as he could. In his fury, his aim was off, and he only got a couple of solid hits in. Before he could get a well aimed third hit in, an iron like grip arrested the movement of his hand containing the rock. The same forceful grasp kept lifting him upward. Matt experienced a second or two of being elevated, then of moving swiftly through the air, before stopping abruptly when he hit the ground. When Matt looked up, he saw Bobby, inches away, glaring menacingly into his face, holding his wrist.

"Why would you stop me Bobby? I could have finished him off. He would be dead. We could take his body out in the ocean, and dump him. He would never be found. It would be over, let me finish it now, for God's sake." Matt pleaded.

"What's happened to you Matt? What's wrong with you? Why would you want to kill Greg?" Bobby shouted the question.

"Don't you see how evil and how conniving he is? He tells lies about everything. He distorts the truth. He tries to ruin peoples lives. He is always coming in between you and me." Matt spluttered.

"What do you mean, coming between you and me?" asked Bobby, with a startled expression.

"You know, you must know, I care so much for you, much more than most people care for their close friends. You must know how much I like you? I don't even want to do all this stuff if you are not here. You must know how I feel."

A second later he added,

"I care so much for you, and Greg was always getting between us. Remember, when I saw you two together that time. That hurt me. He was always trying to turn you against me. That's why he needs to die, one way or the other, he needs to be gone from here. Help me do it now, and we can go on living and enjoying our lives, without him interfering."

"No! Matt, you're wrong. I don't want to get rid of Greg. I like him, and I want him to be here. There is something wrong with how you think. You need to know this about yourself. You are sick in the head. You need to get help. Don't you ever dare to touch Greg again."

Bobby said this with a grave, and deadly serious expression on his face. He then waved a clenched fist in Matt's face.

He turned toward Greg, who was still trying to stand up. Tommy was now by his side; helping him get off the ground. Tommy and Bobby then helped Greg get up and back to the house. Bobby kept glancing over his shoulder to check on where Matt was.

Over the next day, Matt kept to himself. He did not talk with anyone unless he was asked a direct question, and he answered those questions curtly as possible. He made a trip to town by himself. The following day his parents arrived. Just before Matt got in the car, he looked at the three boys. He had a look of determined madness on his face when he said,

"I am going to get even with all of you for turning on me. You will regret what you have done to me, I will make sure of that."

He got in the car, and his parents drove Matt away with them. The parents not saying a word to the other boys.

When Skipper arrived the next day, the boys were filled with sadness and disappointment, as they told him what had happened with Matt.

"That's really bad news. Nothing good can come out of this. But with Matt behaving that way, and expressing that kind of attitude and that way of thinking, it would not be possible for him to be here any longer. You boys are too good and honest to be exposed to that kind of distorted, sick thinking and dangerous behavior. We have all done the best we could for Matt. We certainly treated him like an equal. We do that because that is who we are. It's clear now that Matt was not like us at the end. Something happened to him and it altered his way of thinking and feeling. That night of his almost drowning he definitely demonstrated paranoid type thinking when he accused Greg of trying to hurt him. From what you tell me, he clearly developed a stronger sense of unrealistic attachment to Bobby. Something akin to admiration and misguided love. It is also obvious now that he developed a type of hatred for Greg. This may be an example of how jealousy can alter someone. It was a strong enough emotional attachment that he was ready to kill for it. It sounds like he attempted to do it with the bait bucket, and then definitely with the rock. We did the best we could for Matt, unfortunately it wasn't good enough. We will get along without him. Maybe one day we will find someone else to take his place; someone who really enjoys living here and at the ranch; someone who truly likes all of us." said Skipper.

PART 5

CHAPTER 48

THE PRESENT

It was now two months since Matt tried to kill Greg. It was a Monday morning. The other two boys were already at home, having been dropped off by Skipper, after a weekend at the ranch. Skipper was dropping Greg off at his house. There was a strange car in the driveway. Skipper expressed a concerned interest in whose car it could be. Skipper told Greg he would call and check in with him later that evening. Skipper did not call that evening, nor did he ever call again. Greg never saw the Skipper again.

ANOTHER INTERVIEW

It was eight thirty on Monday morning, and Greg was sitting in his homeroom class at school. It was now almost eight weeks since Skipper had dropped him off at his house that Monday morning, and the FBI agents were at his house. He had not heard from Skipper since that morning, and had not had any communication from any one about Skipper, the ranch, the boat house or the boat. He had just been nominated for president of the class, for the upcoming year, along with two other classmates. This was his third year of being in the same homeroom with many of the same classmates. It was time for the classroom elections for the upcoming year. Greg was not terribly surprised to find himself nominated for class president. He did not think of himself as a leader, but he knew he was liked by almost everyone in the room. He was a better than average student as far as scholastics were concerned. He liked almost all of his classmates, and was on a friendly basis with every one. The class teacher was telling the three nominees for president that they needed to leave the room while the voting was carried out. As Greg was standing up to go out in the hall with the other two nominees, a messenger from the principal's office entered the classroom with a note requesting Greg to report to the principal's office immediately. As he approached the door to leave the classroom, he turned and waved to his classmates, and flashed a big smile.

When Greg entered the principal's office, he was met by the principal who was sitting at his secretary's desk. The principal immediately stood up and said,

"Greg, there are two men from the United States Government who want to speak with you in private. They are in my office waiting for you. You can go on in now."

When he entered the room, he was met by two men he had never seen before. They remained seated and the first man asked,

"Are you Greg Saunders?" When Greg said he was, the same man said,

"Shut the door behind you, and have a seat over here. I am Mr. Bailey and this is my partner Mr. Cooper. We work for the FEDERAL BUREAU of INVESTIGATION. It's a branch of the federal government that investigates crimes."

Greg looked from one to the other, and said nothing. He knew that this must have to with Skipper, since the other two men he met did the same kind of thing. Mr. Cooper who was wearing a cast on his left wrist and hand, spoke next.

Greg, we're here to ask you some questions about the man you know as Skipper."

"O.K." said Greg.

"We are here because there have been some complaints about him."

Greg looked at each of them in the eyes and said,

"It's hard for me to believe that anybody would complain about Skipper."

"Well there have been some complaints, and they are very serious complaints. We need to ask you what you may know about these complaints." said Mr. Bailey.

"O.K." said Greg.

"Then let's get right to it. These complaints are not nice to talk about, but we have to get all of the facts. These complaints have to do with this person Skipper touching one or more of the boys on their private parts. That is against the law, and it is our job to determine if the law was broken. Do you understand what I am saying?" asked Mr. Bailey.

"Yes sir." said Greg

"Good, then let me start by asking you if you were ever touched on your penis or anywhere else on your privates?" asked Mr. Bailey.

"No sir." said Greg.

"What! You are saying you were never touched on your privates by Skipper?" asked Mr. Bailey.

"Yes sir." said Greg. Mr. Cooper then spoke up, and

"So Greg, you were never touched on your privates? Is that what you are saying, because we heard that you were?"

"That is what I am saying sir, and I don't care what you heard. I have never been touched that way." said Greg.

"What do you mean by that way, that sounds like some sort of an evasive answer?" asked Mr. Cooper, who now leaned more forward in his chair.

"Well, that way. Like you are trying to say. Like something wrong was done."

"Well then, did he ever touch you in any way, on your privates?" asked Mr. Cooper.

"No sir. He did not touch me in any way. He never touched me or any one else that I know of. He would never do anything like that. He is too nice a man to do anything like that." said Greg.

"Yes, we understand what you are saying, and I think we now know how you feel too, but we do have a few more questions for you."

"Alright." said Greg.

"Did he ever put his penis in your rectum?" asked Bailey.

"Did he do what?" asked Greg.

"Did he ever put his dick into your ass hole?" asked Mr. Cooper, with a different tone to his voice, and a hint of sternness, on his face.

"No sir, he did not." said Greg emphatically.

"Did you ever touch his penis? Did you ever touch Skipper's penis?" asked Bailey.

"No sir." said Greg.

"Have you ever touched another boy's penis?" asked Cooper. Greg thought about this for a few seconds, and said, "Yes sir. I have done that."

"Will you please tell us about it; when, where and with whom?" asked Bailey.

"O.K., It has happened two times in my life. Once when I was twelve years old. I was with my cousins in Georgia during the summer when I was up there." said Greg.

"Would you please tell us about any other times, when you were not with your cousins in Georgia?" asked Bailey.

"All right, a friend of mine and I touched each other off a couple of times." said Greg.

"When was that?" asked Bailey.

"About six months ago."

"What was his name?" asked Cooper.

"His name is Jack, Jack Simpson. He is a friend of mine from school. He is not in the scouts, and he has never been to the ranch." said Greg.

"Was there another time, with another person, you haven't told us about?" asked Cooper.

"No!"

"Do you think of your self as a homosexual? Are you, you know, like a queer, or a fag, that kind of thing?" asked Bailey.

"No, I do not think I am a queer." said Greg.

"Why not? You just said you have played with boys in the past." said Mr. Cooper, with a straight face.

Greg had been feeling himself becoming more and more irritated at this line of questioning, and now, even more so with this last question. So far these men from the government had only made insinuations about Skipper and now himself. The more he thought about it, the more irritated and the madder he became. Then he pulled his emotions together and calmly said,

"I don't think of my self as a queer. And, here is why not? Because the only thing I think about day and night, is girls, and what a beautiful and mysterious thing they have between their legs. You know what I'm talking about, I'm sure. It's those parts of their genitalia that we boys like to call a p—y. It's really the outside of the vagina, and those lip like pieces of tissue that adorn the opening. You see, I think about those kinds of things all the time. So far I have only heard what they are like; about how soft and warm, and slippery and gooey they are, and then I want to start playing…and sticking my fingers—."

"O.K., O.K., That's enough of that kind of talk." said Bailey abruptly

"Well, you are the one who asked the question, sir. You do want to know the truth, don't you?" asked Greg with an inner feeling of satisfaction. They apparently did not like his snippy and graphic answer, he thought.

"We don't need to hear that kind of descriptive language." said Cooper.

"O.K., but that's why I don't think I'm a queer. What did you want to hear?

That I only like boys, and that I only want to touch a boy's penis. Well, it's not true. I like girls. I only want girls. My only problem now is that girls don't want me yet."

"I didn't really mean to insult you with that last question. I apologize if you took it the wrong way. And to be clear, we don't WANT to hear anything but the truth." said Mr. Bailey.

"I did take it the wrong way, as you put it. Because I am not a queer, and neither is Skipper. Can you tell me where Skipper is? I haven't heard from him." Greg suddenly asked. He watched as the two government men looked at each other. They were obviously not sure of how much information to share with him.

"He is being detained, until the trial. So you will not be hearing from him. Let's get back to our questioning of you." said Mr. Cooper.

"O.K., but can't he get out on bail, or something like that." said Greg.

"Skipper as you call him, is in the military; things work differently in the military. Now listen, we want to get this perfectly clear. You are saying that Skipper has never touched your private parts, and you are sure of that?" asked Cooper.

"Yes! That is what I said. He has never touched my private parts. He has never done anything wrong like that. He would never do that. He is one of the best people I have ever met." said Greg.

"Are you going to testify to that in the trial?"

"Yes, of course, I will testify to that."

"That's all of our questions for now, so you can go back to your classes." said Mr. Bailey.

On his way back to his homeroom, Greg reflected on his use of the word "adorn", he had just learned it in vocabulary studies. He was hoping he had used it correctly when describing female anatomy to the two men. He would have to check on that. He was also thankful that Skipper had told him all about the anatomy of girls. It sure came in handy in his answer to them.

When Greg entered the classroom after his interrogations were over, he was greeted with applause and the news, he had been elected president of the class room for the year. ' Maybe that is a good sign; things might be taking a turn for the better.' he thought.

CHAPTER 49

WAITING, HOPING—and A DILEMMA

IT WAS NOW SEVERAL weeks since the morning the F.B.I. had interviewed him; there was still no communication from Skipper, nor anyone else. Greg was still hopeful that things would soon get resolved, and they could all get back to the ranch, and the boat. He was missing Skipper, the Parkers and the other boys. For him, the weekends were now back to being boring and quiet around his house. On Sundays his mother and stepfather were home. They all three had breakfast together. Greg would then spend the rest of the day doing his homework, reading books from the library, and taking walks around the block. His life was now back to how it had been before he ever became a scout. He no longer went to the scout meetings. He did not even know if they had meetings now since Skipper was no longer the scout master. He spent much of his time daydreaming, and remembering how much better his life was when he was at the ranch and on the boat. He frequently had dreams about the ranch, of being on the boat out in the Gulf of Mexico, of watching the mysterious Gar swimming freely around in the grotto in front of the house. He had one dream that the large fish used under water tunnels to connect their grotto with other distant grottos, or more shallow waters, where they were supposed to be, thus solving the mystery of why they were there, in such deep water.

One evening his mother said, "Greg, I got a call from the F.B.I. to day. It was the men who questioned you. They want to know if you are definitely going to testify in court when Skipper goes to trial. It's a decision only you can make. You are the one who will have to take an oath on the bible, and tell the truth in court. Do you want to think about it a while longer, or do you want me to give then an answer right now?"

Greg had not expected this to be happening so soon. He was not ready to give an immediate answer. This would require some more serious consideration on his part. The part about swearing an oath on the bible in court was what stopped him from giving an immediate answer.

"I want to think about it some more first Mom."

"That's O.K. son. This is your decision to make. Take your time, and let me know what you want me to tell them."

From that moment on, Greg could think of nothing else. He knew he would do almost anything to help get Skipper out of jail, and out of this situation; almost anything, anyway. He had also been thinking about what must have happened to cause this mess. Matt had certainly been very mad and terribly upset after their fight. He said he would get back at all of us, if it was the last thing he ever did. Greg now believed he was trying to do it in this way. He had never seen anyone with so much hatred in their eyes. It was as if the hate was coming out of his very soul. It was as if the devil himself was looking at him through Matt's eyes. He could not believe Matt would hurt Skipper this way though. Skipper had done so much for Matt over the time he was at the ranch and at the boat house. He had even helped save Matt's life that time when he would have certainly drowned. "Too bad he didn't drown that day. None of this would be going on. We could all be back on the boat. We could be out in the Gulf of Mexico, away from all these evil people who claim Skipper is a bad person." he said out loud to himself.

But, what should he do now? Matt had told him he pretended to be asleep, and had witnessed Skipper demonstrating how to wear the jock strap that night. So he had seen and heard what went on between Skipper and Greg. Strictly speaking Skipper had actually touched his testicles and his scrotum. Greg knew this was a true fact. If he went to court and swore on the bible, he would have to say it did happen. God had witnessed what had happened, just like Matt claims he did. God knew the truth. Greg knew he could not tell a lie after taking an oath on the bible, because God would know it was a lie. So if he told the court what had happened, it would be proof that Skipper did touch him on the genitalia. If he did not go to court, they could not make him say anything bad against Skipper. Then they would never know what Greg knew. Greg felt in his heart that Skipper was without a doubt the best person he had ever known in his life. He believed Skipper would never do anything to hurt him, nor anyone else. But then if he did not go to court, he would not be doing anything to help Skipper. This was a bad situation. It was without a doubt the worst situation Greg had ever been in. It seemed to Greg that no matter what his decision, it would not look good for Skipper. If he told the truth, it would be certain proof of Skipper's guilt. If he did not go to court, it would also look bad for Skipper, because they would all think he was guilty because Greg refused to testify. This was awful, that damn Matt had done this; all because of his jealously and hate for Greg. Because of Matt, Skipper was in prison now. If he is found guilty he could be in prison for a long time, maybe forever."

"I have got to think this thing through. There has to be a solution. There is always supposed to be a solution to every problem. Killing Matt, that would be a solution, but I can't do that. That would be worse than lying in court." he said to himself.

CHAPTER 50

MESSAGE FROM GOD ????

ONE DAY, A WEEK later, it was after school and Greg was alone at home thinking about his situation. He wanted to be away from this responsibility. He wanted to be on his boat. He wanted to be away from all this. He felt like he had no one left in his life he could talk truthfully to about difficult problems. He had become so used to being able to talk to Skipper about any difficult issues that were not clear to him. Skipper had a way of making the answer seem so obvious and simple, but he was not available now, and may never be again. Greg suddenly felt a sensation of fear, of being alone, isolated and helpless. How was he going to be able to manage without Skipper. Who could he turn to for help? Who could he ask for help? Suddenly an idea flashed in his mind.

How would Jesus handle this situation? He was God's son. He would know how to make the right decision. "Yes, that's it, I'll ask God for his help." Greg said out loud.

Greg looked into the bathroom mirror. He wanted to check his appearance before talking with God. As he looked at his image, he was thinking about what he had been taught, man had been made in God's image. He wondered if God looked anything like he did. He concentrated hard on what he would say to ask God's help. As he was formulating his words, he sensed a darkness descending outside the house. He then began to hear raindrops on the roof and then large drops began splashing against the windowpanes.

The rain steadily increased in volume.Greg then saw that it was becoming much darker outside, and in seconds it became dark inside the house. Progressively it became darker and darker, and Greg felt a need to turn on a light. As he reached for the light switch, a brilliant, blinding white light flashed, and illuminated the image of himself in the mirror. There was a bright halo of shimmering light around his head, and then his body; then the light intensified and became so brilliant he felt compelled to shut his eyes, for fear of being blinded. He could feel the house shaking as the thunder began.The deafening sound was so loud he wanted to cover his ears with the palms of his hands. He immediately dropped to the floor, on to his knees, his eyes still closed tightly against the intense brightness of the light, his palms pressed hard against his ears. He perceived a bright flickering through his closed eyelids. The continuous roaring sound now changed and started coming in waves.Then gradually and slowly subsided, over the next several minutes, until all was again in total silence. Greg stayed on the floor for several minutes. He opened his eyes and removed his hands from his ears. He pushed himself off the floor and stood up. He looked around to see if the house was still standing. He was surprised to find nothing altered or changed about the house. The event had been so profoundly different from anything he had ever experienced before. He looked into the mirror again to check himself. Surely, he must have been altered in some way, he thought, but he could detect nothing different. He suddenly felt the need to lie down or sit down. He walked to the couch and sat down. He leaned back, and took a deep breath.

After several seconds of sitting on the couch, he began thinking about what had just happened to him. His mouth felt dry. He wanted something cold and wet. Outside, the rain subsided, and the day's light came back to normal. Sitting on the couch, sipping on the iced water, he could hear a mocking bird, close by, begin to sing it's recurrent refrain, over and over and over.

He was deep in thought, trying to analyse the significance of what had just happened. What was he doing when the storm happened? He was about to begin asking God for help in finding the right answer too his questions. Maybe that unbelievable intense and erie light and deafening sound of thunder was God sending him a message. It was certainly no ordinary thunderstorm. He had never tried talking directly with God. If that was God sending him a message, he immediately decided that he should talk to him in person in the Catholic Church.

"If that was God sending me a message, I should talk with him right now. I will take a bus into town, go to the Catholic Church, and pray to God. Maybe it is not enough to just be a good person. Maybe I should have been praying on a regular basis, like when I was in boarding school. Maybe if I had done that, none of this would be happening. I wish I had Skipper here with me now, he would know what to do, he always did." he said out loud.

When Greg arrived at the Church, he was reminded of how magnificent and beautiful it was." It is a fitting tribute to God." he thought.

He had never been in such a large church. When he entered, he could see there were several individuals sitting or kneeling in pews. They were all separated from each other. It was as if they were seeking privacy for their praying. After entering the church doors, Greg stepped up to the container of holy water. He dipped his fingers in, and made the sign of the cross against his chest, just as he had done hundreds of times before.

"In the name of the Father, the Son and the Holy Ghost." he said out loud as he made the sign of the cross. Greg chose a row of seats where there was no one else praying. He wanted to be as far away from others as possible. He chose a pew, entered, and moved half way across, and sat down. He looked around at the huge, softly lit interior. It suddenly all became very familiar to him again. He had gone to church and Mass at least twice a day, and often even more, for the three years at the Catholic boarding school. This church was hundreds of times bigger than the chapel where mass was held at the convent. It was very impressive and overpowering in the way it made him feel. There were dozens of vaguely familiar statues in various locations. They were located around the periphery, in ·oves and in front of the church near the altar. Many of them were like old friends, from his many years of seeing them daily. Greg suddenly felt a sensation of being overwhelmed. After all, he was in the presence of the most powerful spiritual forces in the universe. He had heard about the holy trilogy through out his life. Now he felt the presence of God, his son Jesus Christ and the Holy Spirit, they were here, with him now, they were here in the church. He had come here to ask God alone to help him make the right decision about what to do. But, if all three of the trilogy were here, then so much the better. He spent the next several minutes looking around and feeling the magnificence of his surroundings. He observed the architecture and the beauty of the statues and the paintings. He could see that the tapestries and the colours of the interior of the church were intensified and enhanced by the columns of light coming through the Multi coloured windows. The windows were high up, just below the ceiling. It was comforting to him and made him feel he had done the right thing by coming to God's house to talk with him directly. After all, he was the one asking for guidance in making the right decision.

He moved down to his knees, and bowed his head. He closed his eyes. He let his mind begin to formulate his questions. He felt even more certain now that the blinding light and deafening sound he had experienced from the heavens was God sending him a message. Now that he was in the church and praying; he felt a sense of relief. Now he had someone to talk to again that he could trust. He missed Skipper. He was afraid he would never see him again. He badly needed someone to share his confused thoughts with, some one he could ultimately trust to help him, and guide him in the right direction. As he thought, he spoke quietly, almost in a whisper, but he spoke the words, because he wanted to make sure it was easier for God to hear him, and to know exactly what was on his mind. He then began to talk with his God.

"Dear Father, Son, and Holy Ghost, I am here today to ask your guidance in seeking the right answers to my questions and my problems."

PART 6

CHAPTER 51

TALKING WITH GOD

"Dear God, please help me! I find myself in a strange and difficult situation. I have a good friend. He is the best friend I have ever had, and the best friend I can ever imagine having. We have been friends for more than two years. He would never do anything wrong. But he has been accused of doing something terribly wrong. A boy named Matt claims he saw Skipper touching my privates. He did touch me, but he did not do anything wrong. He was showing me how to wear a jock strap so that it would protect my balls, I should say testicles, I'm sorry God, I'll try harder to use the right words when talking to you. I had never worn a jock strap before. I never needed one because I never played sports. Skipper showed me how to push my testicles up out of the way, so they would not get hurt. Well, Matt claims he saw this happen. He told his parents and they told the F.B.I., and now my friend Skipper is in jail for touching my privates. Now, here is my problem, he did touch me, but he did not do any thing wrong. If I admit he touched me, it proves Matt was right, and all these people think it is very terrible and very wrong for him to touch a boy there. If I go to court, I have to take an oath on the bible. If I say he did not touch me, that would be a lie. I cannot take an oath on the bible, and tell a lie. If I say he did touch me, then it makes him guilty.

So far I have told everyone he did not do it, but I have not been under a bible oath. I don't understand why they all believe it is so bad, if a man does touch a boy there, but they sure do, because there have been four men from the government talking to me about it. My mom and stepfather all act like it is something terrible. It is all so confusing to me. He did touch me, showing me something helpful. I was the one who was touched on my privates. It didn't hurt me, or cause me any harm, or make me feel bad. I didn't get a disease, and I didn't get any one pregnant, which I know now can be a bad thing to do. It did not bother me in any way. I never even gave it a second thought, until all this happened. If Matt had stayed asleep, no one would have ever known about it. What I mean to ask you God is, why does every one besides me think it is so wrong. If it is wrong, why don't I feel bad? Why didn't I have pain, or feel like I was hurt. It makes me wonder if all these people know what they're talking about. I did not get hurt. They did not get hurt. No one got hurt. What makes it so bad? That is what is confusing me. If it didn't bother me or hurt me, why does it bother them so much? They say he will go to prison for doing it. I don't want him to go to prison, but I don't want to tell a lie either. That would be wrong against you God. I never want to do anything wrong against you God. I have heard all my life that a person cannot tell a lie after swearing on the bible. They will even put you in jail for doing it. Every one agrees how wrong it is. I agree it is very important, and I would never do anything against you God. But so far it seems to me that what ever I do, I cannot do the right thing, and some body is going to get hurt. That is the reason I am here talking to you God. I don't want to do anything wrong, but it looks like I can not do anything right. It seems like a bad position to be in, not being able to do what is right. That seems wrong to me.

I don't think Matt is a good person. I think he is the one who is doing something wrong. Strictly speaking he is not telling a lie, because what he says he saw, did happen, but he is trying to make people believe something wrong happened, when he knows it did not. So, as you know he is the one telling a lie.

I know he is trying to hurt me, because he said he was going to hurt me. He does not like me. I know that, he said so. As you know he tried to hurt me really bad when he was hitting me in the head with the rock, he wanted to kill me, and he might have killed me if it had not been for Bobby stopping him. I have never done any thing bad to him. As far as I know or can remember, I have only tried to be a good friend, both kind and helpful to him, but he doesn't like me, and he is trying to hurt me a lot, this time. My life has been going so well for such a long time, ever since I met Skipper, and have been in the scouts. I have learned so much about so many things, and have made many new friends. I thought that my new, good life, must have been a reward from you, like a present or something for me being such a good person. I talked with Skipper about you God. We talked about how you must feel about boys masturbating. He did not believe that you felt it was wrong, and after talking with him and thinking about it more by myself, I didn't think you believed it was wrong either. How could it be? Almost every boy I have ever known does it. That is why I am so confused. No one I know who has done it, has been a bad or evil person except for Matt.

If I were older, I would rather be with girls. Every body I know now, who does it, would rather be with girls. But so far, girls don't want to be with us. So we are spending our time until we grow older and find girls who want to be with us. Please don't think I would ever do anything bad to a girl God. I learned from Skipper about how inconsiderate some boys and some men can be to girls and women. Those kinds of guys are just being selfish. They lie about their intentions. They don't or won't put on a rubber and they risk getting a girl pregnant or giving them a disease or even catching a disease themselves. I would never do anything like that to a girl. I like them, and I respect them and you far too much to do anything bad to one of them. Since you are the one who made girls, they must be important to you, and if you made them, they deserve the same respect. I will always honor everything you made, and give them the respect you intended for them to have. So now God, please, I want to go back to my problem. I need you to help me find the right answer. I have tried to be as good a person as possible; ever since I stopped wearing my scapular. I thought that if I was as good as that, then if I died, I would not have to sit in those fires of hell, with them burning me for eternity. Eternity! a word you understand because you created it; but many of us humans cannot conceive of it. I guess it is the same for any one who dies, they have to face your eternity from then on. Here I go again, getting away from the real problem I came to you for. Please help me find the right answer. I don't want anything bad to happen to Skipper, and I don't want anything to change in my life. My life at the ranch, on the boat, and fishing with Skipper and the other boys, has been the most wonderful life I could ever imagine. It seems like it is good for all of us, being together and sharing. Maybe not for Matt anymore, because he is not happy when he is there with us. If he doesn't like us, why can't he just stop coming to the ranch, and not do what he is doing? Now it looks like none of us will ever get to go back to the ranch again, or the boat house, or be on the boat again. What makes a person want to hurt other people, and take away their happiness. What could be the reason? Is it because of his hate for me? Is it for revenge? I never did anything to harm him? Was he trying to do the right thing in his mind? Could he be trying to protect the other boys and himself from Skipper? I don't think so, he really liked Skipper and Bobby; Maybe even loved them both. Maybe he was jealous. Maybe he felt if he could not be number one, then no one else could be either. If that is the case then he really is crazy. Is it possible that Skipper was touching the other boys, or doing things I did not know about? Is it possible Skipper was doing things to me that I do not remember? That F.B.I. man asked me if Skipper ever put his penis in my anus. Where did he ever get that idea? What would make him think to even ask such a question? I told him right off that nothing like that ever happened. It is interesting, now that I am talking to you, I remember having some strange dreams, but I have those kinds of dreams all the time. Do you think it's possible God, that something like that could have happened to me, and me not know it was happening. You would think that if something like that were going on with the other boys, some one would have said something about it, because we were all very close to each other. We were really close. I think someone would have said something, if there was any thing to say. If strange things were being done to me, and I was aware of it, would it hurt me or upset me? How would I feel about that? What would make it wrong for me? I think it would have to cause me some kind of pain, or discomfort, some kind of damage, physically or mentally, something that would be a constant reminder that something bad happened to me. If I experienced none of those things, then what makes it wrong? How would I know it was wrong? I have no bad memories. There is nothing wrong with me, anywhere. So where is the wrong? How did it become wrong? What makes it wrong? Who is it that is hurt? Is it the person who was supposed to have been hurt, or is it the persons who thinks and believes somebody else was hurt. How do they know somebody was hurt, if there is no evidence they were hurt? If I were to imagine, in my mind, that he played with me, I think I would feel the same way about it. I have let an other boy do it, and I do it to myself. I even want girls to do it. I sure hope that is not going to be bad and wrong too, when that time comes. So I ask myself again. Where is the wrong to me? If there is no pain; no damage, no hurting, nothing, only feeling good. I come right back to the same answer again and again. What makes anything wrong? I think a person has to be wronged, or hurt in some way. I guess causing some one to be jealous is causing them pain, but that is mental or psychological pain, and who actually causes psychological pain. Isn't that the kind of pain a person does to themselves? Because that pain is inside of their heads, and their minds? They are the ones who imagine somebody is doing something bad to them. So who is responsible for that pain? Thank you God for letting me talk to you this way. I am trying to find the truth. If Skipper were here, he would help me find it. He had a way of thinking about your problem, then he would ask questions, and when you answered his questions, you would find that you had discovered the solution by answering his questions. I know you can do that too God, but your method of teaching is different. You let people find out the answers to their problems on their own. You do not ask them those specific questions that lead them to the answer. I don't mean this in a negative way, God, but Skipper's way of teaching helped me to find the answers to my problems easier and quicker. I know you have reasons for doing things your way. Everyone knows your way has to be the best way, and you have your reasons. I can only guess it's because the easy way, is not the best way. Maybe if the answer is too easy to find, it is too easy to forget.

I don't know what your reasons are, but I sure could use some help in knowing what the right thing to do is. When I mentioned that I had strange dreams sometimes, it never occurred to me before that they might be connected to this in some way. I have had accident dreams before. I wake up suddenly by having an excitement that makes a wet area. That has happened to me. So is that bad of me? Who is guilty when that happens while you are asleep, in the middle of the night? If I were a catholic, and went to confession, would I have to confess that I had such an event in my sleep? I do not remember having any dreams like that when I was in the boarding school; maybe I was still too young? So if I had a dream that Skipper did something to me in my sleep, would I be guilty of doing something wrong. When I woke up and did not know anything happened, would I be guilty of doing something wrong? Then suppose, I was awake, and I let him do things to me, like when I let one of my friends touch me, am I guilty of being bad also, or is only Skipper guilty of being bad? From my way of thinking, it seems nobody is guilty of doing something bad unless somebody is hurt or feels hurt in some way. Maybe my way of thinking about it is wrong, but as far as I am concerned, it is me doing the thinking about me, not somebody else doing the thinking about me or for me. I am the one who is supposed to be hurt or injured, so if I am not hurt or injured what gives them the right to say I am. Those F.B.I. agents said that if he touched me, it was a crime, and Skipper would go to prison. So they think it is so wrong, it is a crime. Oh! I just had another thought. Maybe Matt dreams up this stuff because of his brain injury. He has been a different person since he fell of the truck. Maybe that's the reason he dislikes me so much. Maybe the brain injury changed his way of thinking somehow, and he doesn't see the truth anymore. What ever his reasons, he wants to hurt many people now. God, I think the devil got into his soul when he was in the hospital; because that is the kind of thing the devil would do. That is why I think the devil got in to him. It makes me want to hurt him, and I know that it is not right. I am supposed to turn the other cheek, like your son Jesus said to do, but that is not how I feel. I guess me not wanting to do the right thing, and turn the other cheek, is more work of the devil.

Anyway dear God, thank you for listening to me. I hope you are not too busy running the universe, that you can't find the time to help this one boy, find the truth and do the right thing. One more thing, please, I want you to know how I feel about Skipper. Even if he did do something they don't like, I mean even if anything happened, it would make no difference to me, because I was not hurt. He would not hurt anyone. He Is the best person I have ever known, and this Matt is one of the worst I have ever known. That's why I think the devil got into him. I don't know if you can do any thing to help get the devil out of him? But if you can, please help him. Thank you God. I hope your son Jesus is not still suffering too much from all the awful things we humans did to him. Thank you God, for listening to me.

PART 7

LIFE AFTER SKIPPER AND THE SCOUTS

CHAPTER 52

A YEAR LATER

IT WAS NOW A year later after his idyllic life at the ranch and boat had ended. Greg was at a football game between his school and another school in town. Greg ran in to Bobby unexpectedly. It was the first time they had met or seen each other since both of their lives had changed so abruptly. They exchanged greetings, and talked awhile about how their life was now that they were living at home again full time. That was when Bobby told Greg about Skipper.

"I guess, by now, you've heard about Skipper." Bobby said.

"No. I haven't heard any thing about him. What have you heard?" Greg asked.

"Well, he's dead. He was killed. It happened within weeks of him being put in prison. They think it was other inmates. Even in prison, other criminals don't like people who are accused of what Skipper was accused of." Bobby said.

Greg felt sick to his stomach. Then he felt anger and hatred welling up.

"How do you know it's true?" Greg asked, hoping there was some chance it was not true.

"My parents told me. They saw it in the newspaper. The trial was mentioned, and it said one of the scouts testified that he had seen one of the boys touched inappropriately, and that some of the boys were doingthings to each other. Skipper was found dead in his cell. He had been mutilated by who ever did it. I've known about it for a long time now, maybe six months. I was sick and mad about it for such a long time afterwards. After a few months passed, I was not as mad and upset about it as I was initially. I'm sorry to be the one to tell you the bad news, Greg. I was certain you had heard about it already." Bobby said.

"It had to be Matt who testified! Skipper never did anything like that to me. Did he ever do anything to you?" asked Greg.

"No. He never did anything like that to me." said Bobby.

"Do you think it was possible he was doing bad things to some of the other boys without us knowing it?" asked Greg.

"I don't think so. I don't see how he could have been doing those things, and us not be aware of it. Somebody would have said something. I think it was all in Matt's mind. He was clearly sick in the head, and was making things up. He said he was going to hurt us. So if somebody testified in court, it had to be him." said Bobby.

"That rotten bastard, and he was the one who wanted me dead, and he would have killed me too, if it had not been for you. And then you saved his life." said Greg.

"Knowing what I know now, I'm not sure I would do it again." said Bobby.

"Yeah, you would. You would have saved his miserable ass from drowning, even if you knew what he was going to do. You are just too good a person. We were all too good, except for Matt. I think maybe he was good too, before his bad luck when he fell off the truck. It seemed like it anyway. He was a totally different person before that accident, but boy did he ever change. Maybe that's how the devil finds a way to get in to some people. It must have happened when he was in the hospital, and in a weakened state. He sure got into Matt, and then he lived amongst us for a while. There were times when you could sense the evil." said Greg.

"People who are evil, and those with evil intentions will always be among us. I think that as long as there are human beings, there will be some evil persons. And, I don't really know what the role of the devil is in all those people." said Bobby.

"You're probably right, but I wish you had been more evil, or less competent that day you saved his life! Our lives would still be good, and Skipper would be with us now." said Greg.

"We are who we are, and good or bad we have to live with it, even when it hurts us." said Bobby.

"We all got hurt this time, and, now we have to live with it. The worst part for me is Skipper's gone. He is gone from our lives forever now." said Greg.

"I agree with you about that Greg. It sure was wonderful while it lasted, and you got to enjoy having Skipper in your life longer than I did." said Bobby.

"I guess we have to be grateful for the time we did have with him. I know I learned about so many different kinds of things from him. Do you remember the time he sewed up the dog. We found the dog on the back porch one morning. The intestines were hanging out. Something had cut it's belly open. Skipper just ordered some salt water to be boiled. We washed all the dirt and leaves off of the intestines, put them back inside the dog. Skipper used fishing line to sew up the cut. Within a week the dog was as good as new." Greg said.

"He was always surprising us with all the different things he could do. There is no question about the fact he was a very special person; a one of a kind. He sure enjoyed teaching all of us boys to be the best we could be." said Bobby

"I think I will remember one thing he taught us until the day I die." said Greg.

"What's that?", asked Bobby.

"That we are never promised tomorrow. That we should always enjoy and appreciate today. That the present moment is the only thing we can be certain of having. We should live every day and every moment as if it could be our last." said Greg.

"Skipper taught all of us many important things." said Bobby.

"You know Bobby, I feel guilty myself about this whole thing."

"Why would you feel guilty?"

"Before the trial took place, I got what I thought was a message from God." Greg said.

"What kind of message?" asked Bobby.

"I was at home one afternoon. I was asking God for his help in knowing what to do about testifying at the trial. As I was beginning to ask him for help to find an answer, the most unbelievable lightening and thunderstorm took place. I have never experienced anything like it. I'm telling you Bobby, it was just too unbelievable to experience it. So I thought it must be a message from God, and that I should go and pray at the church."

"I don't understand. What was your question to God?" asked Bobby.

"I don't think I ever told you about this before, because I didn't think it wasn't important enough for me to even mention it to you." Greg said.

Greg told Bobby what had happened; about Matt seeing Skipper demonstrating how to wear the jock strap. He told him about the F.B.I. questioning him, and how he had said Skipper did not touch him. But, in fact he had touched him.

"So what was your problem? What were you asking God for help about?" asked Bobby.

"My problem was, if I went to court, I would have to swear on the bible to tell the truth. I believed that if I told the truth, it would be proof that Skipper did touch me on the genitals. There was nothing wrong or bad about the way he touched me, but he did touch me. If I said he did not touch me, it would be telling a lie against God. I was hoping God would give me the answer about what to do" said Greg.

"So did he tell you what to do?" asked Bobby.

"No, he never did. Not directly anyway. But I thought, and eventually believed that if there were no other direct message from God, I should know it meant to do the right thing by God. So I did not testify, because I did not want to swear on the bible and then tell a lie. I did not want to tell a lie against God. So it may be my fault Skipper is dead." said Greg.

"I see it now. The only thing I can say about your situation is, you did what you had to do based on your beliefs. As I see it, that was your only choice actually." Bobby said.

"Yes, maybe. But I still feel guilty. It feels like I did the wrong thing. Look at how our lives have changed. We have lost every thing we loved to do, and the person we loved to do it with." said Greg.

"That may be true, but if I remember my history from bible school correctly, many people over many years gave up much more than what you gave up for their beliefs in God."

"Thank's for reminding me. It is true that many people gave their life and the lives of their family for their belief and faith in God. Many people made greater sacrifices over the years. That way of thinking helps some Bobby. You are truly wise beyond your years. I am reminded now that Skipper used to say that about you a lot." said Greg.

"We just talked about this a little while ago, it does you no good to live in the past. One should live in the present, and prepare for living in the future. That is what you should be doing now." Bobby said.

"You are right of course, and I should try to do that." said Greg.

They gave each other a brief, but strong hug; promised to stay in touch with each other, and said good night.

CHAPTER 53

EPILOGUE

A FEW WEEKS AFTER GREG got the news of Skippers death from Bobby, he was still acutely feeling the pain of his loss. He knew now that his hopes for a possible return to his wonderful life at the ranch was over. With Skipper gone, there would never be another day of the life he loved so much. He would never see the boat again. He would never see the lake in front of the house again. He would never fish in the beautiful second lake he loved; with all of the beautiful, pristine wilderness unchanged by the hand of man. That life was now over with, forever. His friendship and relationship with Skipper was over. He believed his love for Skipper would never be over. It was still hard for him to believe it had all ended so suddenly. His perfect life was now only a memory, and that memory was the only way he would ever enjoy those magical experiences again. He would have to visit his favorite places from now on by relying on searches through his memory banks. He did this mostly at night, before going to sleep. He thought much about what happened. He thought about what he could have done differently. Maybe he should have testified at the trial. Maybe it would have made the difference. It would have been his word against Matt's word. Maybe he should not have been so concerned about swearing on the bible. It was only a little white lie, and it would have been for a good cause. Skipper was not guilty of doing anything bad, so he should not have been so concerned about the truth, the bible and God. How could he have foreseen that his choice not to testify would result in Skippers death?

Now that Skipper was gone, Greg felt the pain of finality. It was always with him. His life of joy in the wilderness, and on the boat in the Gulf of Mexico, at such a young age, and the freedom and independence he experienced, was now over. He would forever be grateful to Skipper for the opportunity and the responsibilities that living at the ranch had afforded him. The faith and belief Skipper had shown towards Greg's ability, and his prospects for the future, had allowed Greg to grow within, and mature more rapidly. The many things he had learned from Skipper, in the time they had been together, would be with him now and always, and they would help him as he prepared to move on with his life in the future.

Greg knew now that he would have to make new and different friends, as he made his plans to create a new life for himself. If there was another way to make life as interesting as it had been, he would try to find it. Just as he had found Skipper, he would try to find new people, and new situations, to make his life as worthwhile and stimulating again. Maybe his life had been too exciting. It was always stimulating and educational being with Skipper. He would now have to find someone else to teach him and help guide him into the future. He believed in his heart, he would never be able to replace Skipper; he could only try. He could never have imagined, when Skipper dropped him off at his house that Monday morning, it would be the last time he would ever see Skipper again. And now, the very best person he had ever known and loved was gone from his life forever. He was dead because the truth, Greg believed in was irrelevant to every one that mattered except himself. He believed he had to be true to his faith in God. He had remained true to that faith, and he had lost many of those things that were important and dear to him. His search for the truth was relevant to his faith in God, but irrelevant to his love for Skipper. His loss of Skipper would be a painful memory for the rest of his life.

Greg was determined to somehow make the most of his loss as he forged ahead. He thought back about many of the conversations and discussions he had had with Skipper. He remembered how much emphasis and value Skipper had placed on getting a better education. He was now determined to take advantage of all the advanced courses that would be offered during his time in high school. He would sign up for every course offered as soon as he could. They were free now, so why not take advantage of the opportunity. He would need to study and work harder, but so what; he did not have anything else to do to with his time now. And what was time for, if not to learn more and better prepare for the future. He began to focus on the topics that Skipper talked about the most during their time together. Reading and writing and improving those skills was one of his favorite subjects. Greg remembered that Skipper had said, if one became proficient in those skills, they would never find themselves without something interesting to do. They would never be bored and have idle hands with which to do the Devil's work. He said that learning more, leads to wanting to learn more. Greg could hear Skippers words regarding the library now. "The more information you take into the library, the more information you will take out."

He saw the similarity about learning; the more he learned, the more he would want to learn. He was already feeling more excited and stimulated about the future as he thought about these things.

Greg now made a decision. He would write a book about Skipper one day. He wanted for people who read his story about Skipper to know the truth. He wanted to create a lasting testament to his friend and teacher. He wanted for people to know how much Skipper loved and was loved by those who knew him best.

By making these decisions Greg now realized that he had just taken the first steps, in a positive direction, toward his life of the future. He was already happier now. If he was successful in his goals, and he was determined to be successful, Skipper's philosophy in life would be shared with the world. His legacy would not end with an unjust death, in a prison, by profoundly ignorant persons, for a crime he did not commit. Greg was already becoming optimistic about the future. He now knew that after he learned to write, and mastered the art of writing, the story of Skipper and his message could live on forever. Greg was convinced that the world and the people in it would be better off when they knew the story of Skipper. He would do his best in helping to make the world a better place. If more and more parents were able to learn to be more like Skipper, would that not help the world be a better place? Greg thought it would.

CPSIA information can be obtained
at www.ICGtesting.com
Printed in the USA
LVHW092134040322
712645LV00002B/44

9 781643 145600